# FRUMPY
## MIDDLE–AGED
# M⦿M

*Dispatches From the*
*Front Lines of Motherhood*

# MARLA JO
# FISHER

Prospect Park Books

Published by Prospect Park Books
2359 Lincoln Avenue
Altadena, California 91001
www.prospectparkbooks.com

Distributed by Consortium Book Sales & Distribution
www.cbsd.com

Library of Congress Cataloging in Publication Data is on file with the Library of Congress. The following is for reference only:

Fisher, Marla Jo | Frumpy Middle-Aged Mom
        Humor; parenthood/motherhood; essays; family life
ISBN 978-1-938849-66-4
Ebook ISBN: 978-1-938849-67-1


Edited by Samantha Dunn and Rebecca Allen
Cover design by Mimi Bark
Page design and layout by Amy Inouye, Future Studio
Printed in the United States of America

# ADVANCE PRAISE

"If you've ever heard yourself say, 'No officer, that is not my son,' or had to explain to your kids that Led Zeppelin is not a mineral, Fisher is your kind of gal. Even if you've never said either of those things, Fisher is still your gal. This book has laughs on every page, and as a parent of teenagers, I know you will desperately need every one. I loved it!"
— W. BRUCE CAMERON, *New York Times*-bestselling author of *8 Simple Rules for Dating My Teenage Daughter*

"Now I know why mothering should come with an instruction manual. Marla Jo's take on being single with children is pure genius—and I know genius."
— CATHRYN MICHON, bestselling author, *The Grrl Genius Guide to Life*

"If you miss the real, everyday-life observations of *Roseanne* (which I do), you will welcome Fisher's true and hilarious new book. In fact, you'll probably devour it like a double-stuffed Oreo."
— CHRIS ERSKINE, humoris and author of *Daditude* and *Lavender in Your Lemonade*

"Marla Fisher, aka the Frumpy Middle-Aged Mom, writes us into adventures so real we cannot help but be carried along. Her piercing descriptions of places and people evoke the work of Mark Twain if he were alive today and living in Orange County, California. Her writing style sails across the page, though I find myself occasionally having to pause to giggle over something hilarious before I can continue reading. As a comedian, I appreciate laughter when someone else serves it to me, and Marla is a brilliant hostess of humor. Her book is a feast for us all."
— VICKI BARBOLAK, comedian and television personality

# CONTENTS

# LET ME INTRODUCE MYSELF

HELLO. Welcome to my book, in which I endeavor to impart my vast store of knowledge about how to be a bad mother, travel cheaply, avoid feeling guilty, and have cancer without fear.

Okay, I'm lying about that last part. I am afraid of my cancer, but that doesn't mean it isn't occasionally funny and even useful—for example, when I don't want to stand in a long line behind other people who don't have cancer. Cancer has made me bold, because once you're staring at death, what else could scare you? Certainly not an annoying guy who won't let you cut the line.

This book is a collection of my columns that I started writing twelve years ago, originally to amuse myself and later for the *Orange County Register*, where I work as a reporter. Then my columns went into national syndication, and, lastly, were written for the Southern California News Group, where I still work today.

The column really started when I adopted two little kids out of foster care at the ancient age of forty-six, after I woke up one morning and realized I forgot to have children.

I was a workaholic journalist, who'd covered every beat imaginable in my newspaper career. I typically worked from 9 a.m. to as late as 10 p.m. because that's just how much I loved my job and my colleagues—who tend to be a group of poorly groomed yet lovable goofballs determined to make the world a better place through journalism.

Since I'm also a poorly groomed goofball, I fit right in, so it took me quite a while to realize that, oops, I was suddenly

middle-aged. Not only had I never been married, I also never had kids. This wasn't so much of a concern, because my
mom was raised as an orphan in hardscrabble Texas during
the Depression, and she was separated from her sisters
and literally farmed out to pick cotton, clean houses, and
do other things on farms as a child. After hearing her many
horrendous stories, I'd already determined that I wanted to
adopt siblings in foster care and keep them together.

The only problem was that I had no idea how to be a
mother. Even though the state makes you take parenting
classes before they hand over kids to you, I never got the
manual. Everything was new and terrifying, and, in the beginning, I had no faith that I could keep these kids alive long
enough to formally adopt them, after they moved into my
house as foster children.

Since I already had fallen madly in love with them, this
was stressful. Every day I worried that the social workers
would notice how badly I stank as a mother, and take them
away from me.

Then, I saw a stand-up performance by a housewife
named Roseanne Barr (*yes, in those days she had a last
name*). She snarled at the audience, "If the kids are alive at
5 p.m., I've done MY job."

I decided this was my new mantra. Maybe I fed them
Kraft Macaroni & Cheese instead of kale and quinoa, and
maybe an inappropriate curse word flew out of my potty
mouth a little too often, and maybe I shouted too much
when I should have been quiet, but damn it, I kept them
alive ALL DAY LONG.

When I talked to my friends about this, I was amazed
to learn that the ones who (unlike me) actually were good
moms were constantly tormented with guilt that they
weren't doing enough, just like me.

Every article, TV show, and website exhorted parents

how they could be better caregivers, better dressed, better at their jobs, better home cooks—well, you know the drill.

There wasn't a single source to be found recommending how to be just ordinary, how to drag yourself and your kids through the day without a single injury or incident.

That's when I decided to become the Frumpy Middle-Aged Mom, and to show the world how to be mediocre—or even bad—at parenting, adulting, and all those other things that people seem to expect of you when you reach a certain age.

And you know what? People responded, because the more you care about being a great parent, the more susceptible you become to the massive guilt factory that is our lot today.

I'm happy to say I kept them alive until 5 p.m. every day. I also took them to Egypt and Thailand, Costa Rica and Europe, mostly against their will.

Then a funny thing happened while I was planning the rest of my life and our future adventures together as a family: I was diagnosed with a particularly nasty version of uterine cancer. In the first of a couple of last-ditch efforts to save my life, I allowed the charmless surgeon at my HMO to cut me open and extract items I'd never actually used. My kids were adopted, after all, so all that female equipment—uterus, ovaries, Fallopian tubes, and such—was only used peripherally, as in to produce enough estrogen to keep me from growing hairs on my chin.

Now that I have cancer, the kids are helping me stay alive, or at least getting me another beer from the fridge when I ask for one.

For the sake of my kids' privacy, I called them Cheetah Boy and Curly Girl in my columns. Cheetah Boy because he runs very fast and loves cheetahs; Curly Girl because she used to have beautiful naturally curly hair before she started dyeing and straightening it.

At this writing, they are twenty-three and twenty-one, so I've managed to keep them alive for eighteen years, and it's a complete mystery to me how that happened.

Many people have told me over the years that my kids are lucky to have me as a mom after their birth parents couldn't take care of them. I know their birth mom, and she's not a bad person, but she couldn't stay off the meth long enough to raise them. They had different dads who had their own issues, which I'll tell you about some other time.

Anyway, the day the judge said those kids were mine forever was easily the best day of my life. I'm lucky to have been able to keep them alive all these years, because today they are terrific people and a joy to be around. We had plenty of hard times—especially during the rocky teenage years—but somehow we all got through it.

These are the dispatches from those times.

# 1

# THE EARLY,
# KNOW-NOTHING
# YEARS

## TWO TRASH BAGS, ZERO CLUE

OCCASIONALLY, people will pick up my column in the mistaken belief they are going to become informed about how to raise children. But, really, no one would come to me for parenting advice unless they'd been drinking heavily. As writer Lori Borgman wrote in her book, *I Was a Better Mother Before I Had Kids*, I will tell you a true story illustrating this point, but I come off badly in it, so please keep it to yourself.

When Cheetah Boy and Curly Girl came to live with me as foster children, I knew nothing about raising kids except what I had learned from watching TV, i.e., that they were small, spilled things on your new Stainmaster carpet, loved sugary cereals with cartoon figures on the box and begged for Kraft Macaroni & Cheese every day.

The day that irrevocably changed my life was August 2, 2002. The kids arrived in their social worker's car early in the morning, with two trash bags filled with their meager possessions. Curly Girl's clothes were in good shape. In fact, it looked like someone had been dressing this cute little three-year-old like a Barbie Doll. Cheetah Boy, who was five, had only a few outfits—ripped, stained, and held together with safety pins.

The first thing I did was take them to a big department store and let them pick out their own new sheets and blankets. Cheetah Boy got Scooby Doo, Curly Girl picked Barbie. Then, I decided they really needed some new shoes.

Now, this seems like a very simple task, right? How could I botch that one, unless I let them pick out stiletto heels? Well, read on.

I drove them to a Payless store (remember those?) that is on a very busy street. I parked on the street, opened the driver's side back door for Curly Girl, and helped her down out of the car while Cheetah Boy got out on the other side, onto the sidewalk.

Ignorant of the ways of three-year-olds, I turned my back to lock the car, in full expectation that Curly Girl would calmly walk to the sidewalk and wait there.

Instead, she ran straight into the street, into the path of an oncoming Ford 150 pickup truck.

The driver blared his horn. I turned around, screamed, and ran to grab her. Fortunately, the driver had managed to screech to a stop three inches from her, but he was yelling out the window at me. "Marla Jo Fisher, you are such a complete moron, no one should have trusted you with children." At least, that's what I think he said as he gunned the motor and sped away.

I walked her to the curb and just stood there for a moment while I regained the ability to walk, thinking, "I can't do this. I can't even keep these kids alive for one entire day. I'm going to get them killed, or do something so astoundingly unsafe that the social workers will come and take them away."

For six months, as I waited for the chance to legally adopt them, I was convinced virtually every second that I would botch it somehow and the social workers would take them. It seemed that surely at some point, they would figure out that I was pathetically incompetent to take care of these kids, whom I already loved ferociously.

Eventually, along the way, I figured out how to do it. More or less.

In 2003, they became my children forever, a source of great joy—although I do still have those moments when I wonder, "What have I done?"

# BUT WE ALREADY WASHED OUR HANDS

WHEN you tell your kids something every day, 365 days a year, for their entire lives, you would think it would make an impression on them. Well, not my kids, who apparently were busy inventing cold fusion at the time.

I am talking about washing your hands. Now, it would be nice if they washed up when they're dirty, but I don't even require that. I only insist that they scrub their hands for dinner.

You would think that I had asked them to write Handel's *Messiah*. In pig Latin.

The following is an actual transcript of a conversation from our kitchen:

Me:     It's dinner time. Wash your hands with soap.

Them: We washed them already.

Me:     Oh yeah? Let's see.

Them: Well, we washed them in 2007.

Me:     Please wash them again.

Them: Okay, they're done.

Me:     Let me see. Go scrub them again, and this time,
        use soap. In case you're unclear on the concept, the
        objective of washing hands is to get them clean.
        Not just to pass them under the water so the dirt
        looks wet.

Them:  We can't wash our hands. We're out of hand soap in
        the bathroom.

Me:     Take the soap out of the shower right next to you,
        and use that.

Them: Okay, our hands are clean, see?

Me:     Great, so let's eat.

Them: Now let's pet the dog, and then crawl on our hands
        and knees to the table.

# MOMMY, CAN I HAVE A CELL PHONE?

MY KIDS don't actually believe this, but Frumpy Middle-aged Mom survived most of her life without a cell phone. Back in the olden days, when we were trudging miles barefoot through the snow, we couldn't text our friends. We couldn't even check our messages. We just had to use the time to do boring stuff. Like thinking.

My house monkeys, of course, have no interest in contemplation. For years, they begged me for their own phones. By age seven, some kids at their school already had them. Still, I resisted. It seemed to me that a grade-school kid needed a cell phone about as much as a dog needed an electric blanket. Not unwelcome, but certainly unnecessary. Not to mention some recent research that's rather alarming about cell phones and brain tumors.

But finally, last Christmas, after going to the toy store and finding them out of every single sale item I wanted to buy, I weakened and went to Office Depot and found a pair of reconditioned TracFones for $9.99. The kind that you have to buy minutes to use. I bought each of the kids a phone and a card that gave them sixty minutes of calling time.

I thought, okay, that was foolish, but they will lose the phones or break them in about a week and that will be the end of it. I won't have to listen to their imploring voices anymore, because I can just remind them in my sternest voice that *they had phones but they lost them.*

My best friend warned me of dire consequences. "You'll never be able to talk to them again, because they'll be on the phone all the time," she said. "It will be a nightmare."

I wavered, wondering if I was making yet another hideous parenting mistake. But I had already wrapped the phones with great care, in three different sets of boxes, to torture the little weasels when they had to open each layer, only to find another layer. I really wanted to see their happy little mug shots.

Yet I almost felt guilty when I put the wrapped boxes under the tree, wondering if I was doing a bad thing.

Well, you can't imagine the indescribable joy on Christmas morning when they opened those boxes. It was like someone had just said they could live at Disneyland forever. Like Cheetah Boy, age eleven, had been awarded a major league baseball contract. Like Curly Girl, age nine, got twelve pet dogs.

Cheetah Boy even rushed over and kissed me, murmuring "I love you, Mom," something he hasn't done voluntarily since 2005.

I was taken aback. For the next day, they did nothing but play with the phones, study the phones, charge up the phones, pore over the manual, change their ringtones, play with the features, call each other for fun.

I had carefully explained—and they understood—that they had a mere sixty minutes of calling time. And, once that time had expired, they would have to buy any additional minutes themselves.

Greatly to my surprise, they hoarded the minutes like Ebenezer Scrooge. I had expected them to call a friend and use up all the minutes the first day. But not a chance. Within a week, I realized that the kids wanted the cell phones not to communicate, but because they were status symbols.

Also, amazingly, the kids cherished their phones. They didn't lose them. They didn't break them. I'm using the past tense about the phones because, well, Cheetah Boy did leave his in his pants pocket, and it got washed.

He had to buy the next one himself. Curly Girl, on the other hand, cared for her phone so lovingly that I agreed to buy more minutes for her after her time expired, since she hadn't even used up the sixty minutes she'd been allotted.

The customer service for their TracFones, however, was so abominable that I decided we'd get GoPhones from AT&T instead. The clerk at Radio Shack set up the GoPhones for the kids himself, instead of the long agonizing process of trying to set it up ourselves, so I was predisposed to like them immediately. I told the rugrats that if they hoard the 100 minutes I'd just bought them for $25, and they haven't used them all up, when they expire, I will buy them more minutes. If they do use up their minutes, then they can buy them. Everyone seems to think that's fair.

So I have a way to reach the kids in an emergency, they have their status symbols, and it's not costing me an arm and a leg. Plus, it's teaching them responsibility.

That is, when they actually have their phones. Cheetah Boy's phone is in my purse right now. This is the second time it's been taken away at school and I had to go redeem it. This time, he lost it for two weeks. He swore he did nothing. But his gym teacher caught him texting during an assembly.

Sigh—he's almost twelve now. Like a bad acid trip, I feel it coming on and I can't stop it. Soon, he'll be like one of my colleague's sons and sending 40,000 text messages a month. And he'll go blind and his fingers will fall off.

## IT'S LIKE, TOTALLY GROOVY TO ME, MAN

HEY, it's heavy, man. These are things that creaky old moms like me enjoy with our kids, even if younger moms are laughing behind our backs:

**Books.** I was recently on my way into the library when I saw a child walking out, playing his Nintendo DS. I was so taken aback, for a moment I may have stopped breathing.

An entire building full of books, magazines, newspapers, CDs, and DVDs, and this kid has to play his video game? A horrifying glimpse of the future.

**Thank-you notes.** Remember those? Someone goes to a lot of trouble to do something nice for you—maybe buy you a gift, invite you to a party—and then you write and say thanks. What an old-fashioned concept. Maybe someone could teach that to my nieces and nephews, who have never acknowledged receipt of a single gift I mailed them in twenty-two years.

**The Beatles.** My kids know all the lyrics to every Beatles song except "Why Don't We Do It in the Road," which they don't need to learn until they've been married for at least six years. Not long ago, I went into a music store that displays a poster of the famous *Abbey Road* album cover. I mentioned to the young guy working there that I had seen Paul McCartney on that exact spot in London, in his navy blue Mercedes. The guy looked up at the poster and said indifferently, "Oh yeah. I don't know too much about the Beatles." The indoctrination of my children began that very night.

**The Brady Bunch.** I admit it, I tape old episodes of *The Brady Bunch* and watch them with my kids. Marcia, Marcia, Marcia, why tamper with perfection? It's a better show than any piece of Disney Channel tripe, and my kids still love them today. Now, if I could only get Alice to come and work for me. . . .

**Black-and-white movies.** My children act like they are being burnt with cigarettes if I suggest we watch a movie in black and white. Usually, I only prevail when I insist that, after 500 viewings of *Karate Dog*, which is, incidentally, the worst movie ever made, maybe it's time Mom gets to pick a flick, such as *Casablanca* or *The Thin Man*. I showed my kids the tiny black-and-white TV in my bedroom that I bought for five bucks at Goodwill, and they kept asking me,

"Where's the color?"

**Water from the tap.** Don't tell anyone, but I wash water bottles, refill them with tap water, and put them back in the fridge. I just can't stand to waste all those perfectly good bottles.

Occasionally a kid will come over to play and say, "Can I have a soda?" When I announce that we have a choice of water or milk, sometimes they look annoyed and say, "What?! No soda?" I tell them, "If you want a soda, you can have one. Go home and get one."

**Dead Fish.** This is the best game ever invented. Kids lie on the floor and pretend to be dead fish as long as possible, while other kids try to make them move. It's amazingly quiet and peaceful for the five minutes the game usually lasts. You can even get in a power nap.

## THE HELL KNOWN AS CHUCK E. CHEESE

RINGING in your ears? Upset stomach? Headache? You don't need to see the doctor. You just need to get out of Chuck E. Cheese.

Before Cheetah Boy and Curly Girl, I was only vaguely aware of the monstrous mouse.

When Cheetah Boy moved in with me at age five, he begged to have his sixth birthday party at Chuck's. I was happy to do this, first because I'd never stepped foot in the place, and second, because he'd been deprived of so much during his life in foster care, I was itching to make up for some of that. Someone should have just committed me instead.

The first clue to what I was in for was when my next-door neighbor asked if she could just send her son with us, instead of bringing him herself. I should have realized that this was a woman who knew more than I did.

I, on the other hand, innocently called and made a reservation for a Saturday afternoon birthday party, unaware of what was ahead. I won't describe the entire event. Suffice to say that I didn't get to enjoy anything with my son, because he instantly disappeared into a huge roiling mass of children, only to reappear regularly to demand more tokens.

The clanging of the arcade games was loud enough to be heard from space. My friends who arrived quickly dropped their gifts and ran like they were being pursued by Godzilla.

After I had emptied my bank account, I mortgaged my house online and got some more tokens so all the kids could play games. Fortunately, Chuck now has pawn shops right inside his restaurants, so you can hand over the title to your car, pawn your wedding rings and the deed to your house to get enough money to pay for the event. (Just kidding.)

When the cardboard imitation pizza arrived, I, along with the brave parents who were sticking it out with me, went out and with great difficulty managed to cut our calves out from the herd and get them back to the table for pizza and cake.

It's hard to believe, but Chuck E Cheese is actually making its pizza even worse by reducing the amount of real cheese in the cheese. Are you kidding? There's cheese in there? I figured it was some kind of melted Styrofoam product.

Anyway, the great rat himself then made a special command appearance. And what was Cheetah Boy's response? He burst into tears and went and hid in the corner.

That was the high point of the event.

The following year, my son again asked for a party at Chuck E. Cheese, but this time, I was prepared. "I would rather rub ground glass into my eyes," I told him.

Wait a minute—ground glass, maybe *that's* the mouse's secret pizza ingredient!

## THE BACK-TO-SCHOOL BLUES

THE KIDS went back to school last week, and I pretty much knew how the dialogue around our house would go. Our school is only a couple of blocks away, and the kids have been walking there for years. Curly Girl is going into fifth grade, Cheetah Boy into ... seventh. How did that happen? It's scary.

For the first and only time this year, it was easy to get them out of bed and dressed.

Me: Want me to walk to school with you for the first day?

Kids: No thanks, Mom.

Me: I could help you find your classrooms...

Kids: No, we can find our own classrooms.

Me: I could come along and meet your teachers...

Kids: No, thanks. We don't need you. Stay home and work.

Me: But I want to come!

Kids: Yeah, but we don't want you to come!

Me: (Tears running down my cheeks)

Kids: Wait, don't cry, Mom, you can come meet our teachers on back-to-school night. We'll come with you, okay? It'll be okay. You'll be all right by yourself. Right? Mom? Mom?

Yup. That's exactly what happened! Even worse, they were so anxious to get out the door that I had to drag them back and make them kiss me goodbye.

Is this what it's like when they go to college?

## THERE GOES MOM, THE PACK MULE

HEE HAW. Do my ears look like they're growing longer, like Pinocchio's when he ran away?

Because, when you're a mom, you often feel like a pack mule, hauling all your kids' junk from one place to the next.

Sweatshirts, snacks, juice boxes, crayons, coloring books, water bottles, soccer cleats, baseball gloves—it seems like everywhere we go, there's a new stack of stuff to be hauled along. The kids might get cold at the game. They might get hungry at the museum. They might get restless in the restaurant. They might need a spacesuit for a NASA launch.

Maybe they'll get a last-minute invitation to the White House and need a shirt that's not decorated with today's lunch special.

Other people may go for the chic leather clutch purses. Maybe a nice Louis Vuitton handbag. I can only dream, because my purse is a big sturdy backpack.

Pack mule momism is never more evident than when you go on vacation. You spend half your trip packing up your kids, and the other half unpacking them. Recently, I was pondering this as I remembered my two kids packing themselves for their week-long summer camp.

That's right, I said packing themselves. If you teach your kids to pack, then eventually they will learn to do it without you.

Until that time arrives, I can think of some memorable mishaps.

There's  the time I packed and repacked my kids' suitcases three times to make sure they had everything before we got on the plane to Thailand. When we got to the hotel, though, I discovered I had forgotten something: my own underwear.

I hadn't brought a single pair of underwear for myself. Believe me, they don't sell plus-size underwear in Thailand.

After that mishap, I started abiding by the same principle as airplane oxygen masks: I pack my own bag first, then go and pack the kids up. As the kitchen sign says, "If

Momma ain't happy, ain't nobody happy."

I have this wonderful fantasy: Someday, when I'm a really, really old lady, all doubled over with my cane, one of my kids will have a really heavy backpack. It will be full of all my stuff: my sweater, my knitting, my book, my denture adhesive.

And I'll just be walking along, slowly, with a smile.

## FOR YOUR OWN GOOD, NO, WE CAN'T COME TO YOUR HOUSE

HAVE YOU ever felt paralyzed with fear at the thought of bringing your children into someone's home? I always feel like saying, "Sure. Do you have homeowners insurance? Really? How much is your deductible?"

Never believe people when they say, "Sure! C'mon over. And bring those cute kids of yours." They're well-meaning and all, but clueless.

If they have no children themselves, or their kids have been grown for a long time, then they are sitting ducks for the Fisher Family Wrecking Crew.

"Danger, Will Robinson! Danger!" I always want to cry, just to give them a heads-up about what's actually coming for them.

Why not just bring in Attila the Hun and his thundering hordes while you're at it?

Instead, I just bring my clipboard and pencil over and walk around the proposed site like the advance Secret Service crew would for a presidential visit.

"Antiques? Check. Limoges porcelain? Check. Cupboards that can be climbed with a cookie jar on top? Check. White furniture? Check. Hand-blown Venetian glass collection? Check. Visible electronics? Check."

After my inspection, I meet with the homeowner involved. "Here's a list of things that must be put away for their own safety before we can come over," I explain. "And the white couch has to be covered. When you've made the necessary retrofits, give me a call. Or, we can just meet at a neutral location."

Before I had children, I used to wonder why my friends stopped socializing with me after they experienced the miracle of birth. I like kids and being around them. I felt a little slighted that my friends no longer accepted my invitations.

Later, much later, I came to realize that people with young children, like zebras on the Maasi Mara, tend to hang out in packs for safety. Only other parents can be trusted not to run screaming when that pizza that went down so smoothly comes back up—all over the new Berber carpet. Only other parents have the correct arsenal of sippy cups, plastic bowls, duct tape, and sappy G-rated videos necessary to survive the onslaught without casualties. Only other parents won't judge you when they walk into your house and promptly step on a carpet of Legos that escaped from the bin.

I still recall my child-free friend getting into my Toyota 4Runner and recoiling in horror at the Cheerios ground into the carpet, the wrappers and other detritus that my little angels had left in the back seat. "You *could vacuum back here*, you know," she pontificated at me while wiping down the seat before she placed her rear on it.

Now, let me mention that her big yellow Scooby Doo-like puppy, who was like her child at the time, had recently become carsick and thrown up in my purse on the way to Joshua Tree.

I don't mean he threw up on my purse. I mean he threw up in my purse. Yeah. He did. It was disgusting.

So when she said that, I thought to myself, "No, actually I can't because I don't have two seconds left in my day after

I work full time and then come home to be a single mom, but someday you'll have a child and then you'll get a clue."

And, sure enough, she did have a kid, and I'm pretty sure there are ground-in Cheerios now in her back seat.

## ICE CREAM TRUCKS
## ARE THE ULTIMATE EVIL

DO YOUR ears hang low? Do they wobble to and fro?

Well, the answer is yes, because my ears have been bombarded with the ice cream truck's hideous electronic "Turkey in the Straw" 10,000 times this summer, a tune that gets stuck in your head for decades to come. When I adopted my kids, a friend with six children warned me: Never, ever let them buy ice cream from a truck. Otherwise, they'll torment you every day all summer.

Since I truly believe these trucks were sent by Satan to drive people mad, I followed her advice. I don't want their evil dominion to spread.

I wasn't surprised to hear about ice cream truck vendors being arrested for selling drugs out of their trucks. If you will drive around a peaceful neighborhood, blasting loudspeakers and disturbing the peace, you will stop at nothing. Drugs, robberies, murder. It could happen.

Years ago, I lived in a neighborhood where these pests drove through once an hour. They set their speaker volume so loud, and drove so slowly, that you could hear each truck for an hour coming and going. It was like living in a frozen dairy nightmare.

They would stop when a customer came up, and let the songs grind on and on. A city ordinance actually required them to turn off their speakers if they stopped, but they never did.

Getting "It's a Small World" stuck in your head for

hours was like being infected by one of those horrible tropical maggots that enters through your foot, grows and then
bursts out of your brain.

I heard from one reader of my column who mentioned
one way in which the ice cream trucks could be made even
worse: She said that in Cambodia, all the trucks play Christmas carols all the time, despite the fact that it's not Christmas at all, or that Cambodia is a Buddhist country. That
would lead to violence, I think.

A source from Cambodia reports that, actually, ice
cream merchants there push carts through the streets singing *ga ream, ga ream,* or ice cream, which, heard dawn to
dusk, over and over, may trigger throbbing migraines—but
not the fist fights of the kind provoked by "I Saw Mommy
Kissing Santa Claus."

If your kids already bug you to get ice cream, there is
something you can do. Rent the 1995 movie *Evil Ice Cream
Man,* in which an escaped mental patient chases kids and
drives around in his truck, giving kids treats filled with in-
sects and pieces of dead bodies instead of ice cream.

They also made a movie in 2005, *We All Scream for Ice
Cream,* about an ice cream man who came back from the
dead as a bloodthirsty ghost after he was tormented and accidentally killed by neighborhood children.

Show that to your kids, and maybe they'll never beg for
a treat from the truck again. I haven't tried this yet, but I'm
thinking about it. . . .

# I ACCIDENTALLY BECAME
# THE TEAM MOM

SOMEHOW I accidentally ended up as team mom for Curly
Girl's soccer this year, and I'm the worst one ever.

If you aren't familiar with the First Principles of Youth Sports, there's always a team mom—or to be more politically correct, team parent—who has the important yet utterly unpaid job of corralling a dozen or more squirrelly kids and their parents.

The team parent must complete essential tasks, such as getting uniforms, ordering a team banner, signing people up for snack duty, organizing end-of-season parties, finding a sponsor, and making sure everyone shows up for Picture Day, order forms in hand.

In the past, I have avoided this job like the plague. It's a ton of work, and no one appreciates you. In fact, they likely complain about you behind your back. Did I mention that it's unpaid?

This year, however—and I'm not making this up—I accidentally became team mom. I told my daughter's coach I'd go to a meeting, and it turned out to be the team parent meeting. I walked in and was promptly handed a notebook filled with information and a box of uniforms.

Oops. Sucker punched.

So here I am, de facto team mom, and I've been haranguing the parents every ninety seconds to send their daughters to practice with Picture Day forms, so I can have them all early, in advance of the big day.

What is the problem with that? Well, I already lost two forms people gave me. Picture Day is Saturday.

In the panorama of youth sports, Picture Day entails making sure that a passel of kids arrives at a park shortly after dawn and stands there, yawning, until a professional photographer snaps photos that he or she hopes their parents will buy at enormous expense to send to all the folks back home.

That would be enough to make me nervous, except I also just discovered I have to have $150 sponsorship money or we can't do Picture Day at all. Oops again. We have no sponsor. We have no money.

So I just emailed all the parents to tell them they have to bring $11 cash, exact change, to the practice today. I'm sure they are cussing me out. I mean, who has $11 in exact change lying around? You either have to go buy something for cash at the store, or go to the bank. I told them I will be happy to let them do a better job than me. In fact, please do a better job than me.

Another reason I'm a bad team mom is that I can never remember anyone's names, neither the girls nor the parents. This is a bad quality in a team parent.

To be specific, I will likely remember talking to you, and recall that you have a golden retriever and drive a blue Honda, but I will not under any circumstances remember your name or which child is yours.

I will flee in terror before I'm forced to introduce you to someone else. Either that, or I'll just stand there awkwardly, aware that I am being gauche by not making introductions, and hoping desperately that you will introduce yourself so I have a glimmer as to your name.

After the second game, good team moms do not walk up to the girls like I do and say, "Who are you? Everyone seemed to be clapping for you."

They walk up to the girls and say, "Hi, Brittany. I loved it when you did that awesome thing out on the field that I was able to recognize the sheer brilliance of, because I'm not completely ignorant about soccer."

At least, I'm happy to say, I have demonstrated my amazing managerial skills by delegating most other duties to other parents, including the making of the banner and the hosting of the team party. I wish we didn't have to provide snacks. My theory is the girls mostly throw them away anyway. But I'm always outvoted on that point.

The only other task I've ever taken on for Curly Girl's team was ordering the team banner—and I managed to spell the coach's name wrong. This was pointed out to me by another mom. Sigh.

Luckily, the nice people at BannersUSA in Huntington Beach took my frantic phone call, fixed it for me when I brought it back, and didn't even charge me. Thank you.

So if you stop by Curly Girl's game Saturday, please introduce yourself, even if I'm your son's godparent. And if you know where those two missing Picture Day forms are, let me know.

## I WANT TO RUN WITH SCISSORS

THE OTHER day, I was thinking about the famous parental admonition, "Don't run with scissors," and wishing I could do it. Yes, I would like to run with my scissors for a simple reason: That would mean I could actually find a pair.

My house is not bereft of scissors. I know this because I personally purchased 825 pairs in the past year alone. One notable day, when there was a good "back to school" sale, I bought an entire packing crate of scissors, thinking this would take care of my scissatory needs at least until we're all underwater from global warming.

But, you see, I have children.

You parents out there know what's coming next.

That's right. The disappearance of household scissors is an even worse problem, globally speaking, than the launching of socks into outer space, directly from the dryer.

While it's true that NASA satellites have detected millions of mateless socks floating around Earth, apparently launched from dryer exhaust fans, this isn't really such a big problem. After all, you can always wear shoes without socks in a pinch.

But the problem of missing scissors is much more severe. You cannot cut paper without scissors. This means no clipping coupons, no cutting off the bottom of field trip permission slips or endless other crucial activities that can only be performed with this indispensable household tool.

Yesterday, I looked in the drawers where my kids have been instructed 1,823,422 times to place them, and I couldn't find a single pair. I looked in my sewing basket, where I began to hide some after I nearly sawed off my finger trying to break thread without them.

Gone, like the herds of plains buffalo.

Scissors may have been invented 3,000 years ago, and they've been vanishing as long as there have been children, which experts estimate probably appeared around 982 AD.

I was so desperate to find a pair that I found my canteen and compass and mounted an expedition into the inner reaches of my children's bedrooms, using my walking stick to move aside mounds of piled clothing in hopes that a pair of scissors might suddenly appear, or jump out from their captivity.

No such luck.

I went back to my desk and tried tearing the mailing label I wanted to use, but it just looked messy. So in desperation, I went and bought a metal detector. Using the metal detector, and wearing a pith helmet and sturdy boots, I ventured back into my kids' rooms and this time found success.

Not only did I find scissors, but 428 spoons, forks, and knives that started to go missing in 2002, shortly after Cheetah Boy and Curly Girl came to live with me.

I also found a metal letter opener, 8,244 paper clips and every one of the metal hair clasps from my Clairol hot roller set that I threw away in 2007 after it became unusable due to mysteriously missing parts.

Okay, I'm making that up. I didn't really buy a metal detector, but I'm thinking about it.

I guess I should also think about why I let my kids collect so much junk that their rooms become impenetrable jungles, but I'll have to put that on the list, right after "think about why you look at cobwebs on your ceiling but feel no urge to remove them" and "explore why you know you need to get your expensive car tires rotated but don't."

Meanwhile, I've been thinking about the book *Running With Scissors*, a memoir about growing up in a house full of lunatics. Even before I read the book, I already knew what that was like.

Later, I'll be stopping by the dollar store, so I can buy another pair of scissors. Yes, they are cheap and get dull fast. But since they'll spend most of their lives in hiding, does it really matter?

## IF YOUR FRIEND IS TRUE, YOU NEVER HAVE TO ASK FOR A HELPING HAND

ONE USEFUL side effect of bad luck is that it helps you distinguish your real friends from the rest of the pack.

You've likely noticed this yourself: how misfortune or trouble makes your true friends rally around you, while your ersatz friends suddenly lose your phone number and forget where you live.

There are several times I can think of when you have the chance to hoe out those weeds:

• When you move to a new house
• When you get sick
• When you lose your job
• When your car breaks down
• When you need a ride to the airport

I've been told by a few friends to never, ever buy a pickup, because then everyone wants you to help them move.

Well, I've reached the stage in my life where I don't ask for help moving anymore, since most of my guy friends have thrown out their backs 857 times, and most of the gals don't want to ruin their expensive manicures. Hiring professional movers is much more sensible and emotionally satisfying.

I love watching burly men flex their muscles, even when I'm paying them.

However, I do still remember the "friend" I had years ago who kept insisting that I should call her when I was going to move, because she would come over with her truck. I demurred, saying that I didn't want to be a burden. Since she insisted, though, I did actually call her when I was ready to move.

Sorry, my friend said, in a cold, tight voice. She was busy all week, winning a Nobel Prize or having lunch with the pope, or something like that.

The thing that made my blood pressure spike was that she acted put out, like I was imposing on her. This was embarrassing.

In contrast, your real friends are the ones who don't ask, "Do you need any help?" They just show up, with moving boxes, casseroles, a box of tissues—or maybe a loaded .45, depending on the situation.

When I bought my first house, my friend Robin showed up at my old house, defrosted the icebox and moved all the food for me, without being asked. I really appreciated this, because I had reached that point in every move where you hit the wall, and one more task seems simply insurmountable.

Walk across the street for a million dollars? Sorry, I can't lift my legs.

Well, actually I really can't lift my leg at the moment, at least the one with a cast on it, which I broke a month ago.

This has really been an issue, since I'm a single mom.

And, once again, Robin has shown up at my house nearly every day to haul Curly Girl and Cheetah Boy to their endless games, practices, recitals, and whatnot. She has gone grocery shopping. She has even taken Buddy the Wonder Dog to the dog park.

And she is not even legally obligated to do this. Though it's appropriate that she has parachuted in to help, since she has taken up skydiving in her retirement.

So thanks, Robin! And, if you want her phone number, forget it. She's mine, all mine.

## KIDS HEAR THE DARNDEST THINGS

IF YOU have kids, you've already noticed that they have the uncanny ability to overhear everything you don't want them to know. It's a law of physics that children can never hear you say, "It's your turn to wash the dishes," until you holler it at the top of your lungs, standing between them and the TV.

But they can hear from two houses away when you whisper into the phone, "No, really, don't tell the kids, but they took him off in handcuffs."

I used to think I was being clever when I took the phone receiver for our land line into my bedroom and then into my private bathroom, closing both doors, to listen or convey some juicy piece of inappropriate gossip or share a big concern.

Later, I discovered that the kids knew everything being said, since they always picked up the extra receivers and listened in. Duh. Where was Maxwell Smart's cone of silence when I needed it?

It's not just that kids overhear things. It's that they repeat them indiscriminately to everyone they meet on the block, at the grocery store and at school.

Sometimes, they're repeating things they overheard accidentally. And, sometimes, they're repeating things that you, the parent, actually told them, because you were in a drug-induced state or maybe just brain-dead that day.

My daughter, especially, has never forgotten a single thing I've told her since I adopted her, even when I wish she would.

I've learned that these are some things you should never, ever tell your kids:

1. "Stay out of that drawer, Mommy has personal and private things in there."
2. "Yes, Uncle is in jail, but we don't want anyone to know about that."
3. "Daddy's new wife looks like she got her boobs on sale at Big Lots!"
4. "Yes your daddy smoked pot, but he's very sorry now and you should never do it."

And, of course, the all-important single word, "Yes." Never, ever say this word to your child involving any sort of future activity. Always say, "Maybe." As in, "Hmm, maybe you can go swimming, if you get your room cleaned up and do your homework." Or "Hmm, maybe we'll have spaghetti for dinner, if you empty the trash and clean up the dog poop."

And, "Maybe we can go to Chuck E. Cheese, if you stop telling everyone how much Mommy weighs."

## WHY YES DEAR, YOUR MUSIC DOES SUCK

WHEN I became a parent, it hadn't really occurred to me that I would never get to listen to my own music again. I knew I'd have to clean up after kids, cook and shop for them, and spend every waking moment either at a soccer game or chasing a dog I never wanted down the street. But no one warned me that my life would now become dominated by musical tastes of minors.

This all starts early, with songs that you have to ingest in moderation, lest they give you Type 2 diabetes. I'm talking, of course, about any of the vast repertoires of nauseating Disney and *Sesame Street* albums that my kids wanted to hear over and over again in the car. Really, you haven't lived until you've heard Elmo's falsetto voice singing "She'll Be Comin' Round the Mountain" thirty-seven times in a row.

Then there's Dave Kinnoin, whose music was bearable when my kids were of suitable age, though if I had to hear "I'm Just an Itty Bitty Baby" one more time, I was tempted to find ol' Dave and pound him back into the womb himself.

To this day, I don't mind listening to Tom Chapin, who manages to inject a little wit into his songs that even grown-ups can appreciate—like "In the Nick of Time," about how kids have antennae that tell them how to come when called exactly one nanosecond before you blow your cork completely. And his song "Cousins," about the havoc wreaked on the house by a visit from relatives.

In truth, I have begun to wax positively nostalgic about the Tom Chapin years, now that my kids are thirteen and eleven. No more cute songs about making doo-doo and shoveling snow for them. Now, every time we get in the car, they want to listen to Eminem and a wide assortment of interchangeable rappers, none of whom I can remember and all of whom sound exactly alike to me.

Even though I don't like the cussing, I must say I actually prefer Eminem's gritty music to the light teen pop full of voice synthesizers. If I wanted to hear machines instead of the human voice, I'd turn on the vacuum cleaner.

My friend Kim, who raised two sons who are safely launched into adulthood and now has an adopted teenage daughter, tells me that "kids keep you young" because you're forced into an intimate relationship with teen culture every day. I keep trying to remind myself of this, every time the kids grab the remote and change my acoustic music channel to KIIS-FM.

And I also think back to my own parents, who were horrified when I started bringing home Led Zeppelin albums and playing them on the only stereo in the house—in the living room.

I still avoid listening to some of my favorite songs around the kids, like "Friend of the Devil" by the Grateful Dead, or any of the drug-laced musings that epitomized my generation. I recently struggled to explain to my daughter why Arlo Guthrie was "coming into Los Angeles, bringing in a couple of keys" and why he didn't want the customs man to touch his bags.

So far, I'm following Kim's advice, which is not to allow the kids to have electronics in their rooms. That way, there's no reason for them to disappear into their rooms for their entire teenage years, because there's nothing for them to do there except read books. And that ain't gonna happen.

"I always like hearing the kids' music," Kim frequently tells me. "We dance to it together."

Well, I think my children would be horror-stricken if I started dancing in the living room, based on how they act when I even clap my hands. But if I can learn to listen to Justin Bieber without my teeth starting to ache, that will be a good start.

## NAPPING IS AN EXERCISE IN FAITH AND DEMOLITION

TRYING to sleep while my kids were awake was an

extremely perilous proposition around my house, back when the youngsters were still being patted on the head and called "cute" by most everyone they met. In truth, they may have seemed adorable to the outside world, but they could have been licensed as a miniature demolition squad, with their ability to destroy virtually anything in the time it took for me to catch forty winks.

I always pondered the efficacy of duct taping them to their beds as a possible solution, but they'd usually already used up all the tape on the dog. Besides, there wasn't enough sticky tape in the world to keep them from their appointed rounds, once I indicated my desire to briefly lay my head on my pillow.

On any given day, this could include pounding nails into the porch, blasting the fire extinguisher, trying to jump off the roof, disassembling all the staplers in the house, or leaping on top of the car.

Setting them in front of a video did nothing except give them ideas.

Granted, I was rather geriatric in mom years when I adopted my kids, which was right around the same age my classmates were getting grandchildren. Being a procrastinator, it took me that long to get it together. But I have never regretted this decision for an instant, even when the little buggers found all my hiding places for brownies and drank all the milk in the fridge that I was hoarding for my morning coffee.

But chasing around a pair of little kids is not easy, even when you're young. At my age, it wiped me out. I really, really needed my naps. The main obstacle to my glorious dream of napping was my daughter, Curly Girl, who despised sleeping in the afternoon, even as a tiny tot.

When she'd come home from preschool and I'd ask her how her day went, Curly Girl would throw me an accusatory look and say, "We had to take *a nap*," as if somehow it was all my fault for sending her to this hellhole.

Five days a week, she'd trot off to preschool with her little folded beach towel to lie on, but she never slept a wink. Instead, she'd lie there in the gloom, staring at the ceiling and seething, concocting vivid fantasies of how she would someday wreak revenge on the adult world, for the indignity of being forced to lie flat on brushed cotton for hours each week, wasting her life away.

It was the same story at home. After chasing her around all morning, fetching her drinks, making her breakfast and lunch, bathing her, getting her dressed, cleaning up and all the other accoutrements of being a mom, by afternoon, I was done. I needed my nap. And I could theoretically take one.

But the issue was—what exactly was my daughter going to be doing while I was asleep? Her brother sometimes napped, but often conspired with her in schemes designed to drive me into the loony bin.

The one that comes to mind most often began with the knock on the door that startled me awake one otherwise fine afternoon. Our brand-new neighbor, who'd just moved in and I hadn't even met yet, was standing there in all her young, hip, professional architect-ness.

This husband-and-wife pair had been living on a sailboat until their parents bought them this vintage house in the tough neighborhood. They immediately began remodeling it and carefully removing every historic bungalow feature that made it interesting, even though the house had just been remodeled.

"Do you know what your children are doing?" she asked me in an accusing manner, without even saying hello. I had to sheepishly confess that, no, I didn't, because I'd foolishly fallen asleep.

"They're throwing glass onto my driveway," she snapped

and walked away, never looking back.

I hustled into our tiny backyard, where I discovered that the little angels had made up a new game: breaking glass panes out of an old, disused window leaning up alongside the storage shed, and throwing them over the fence to hear the satisfying crash on the other side.

As you might guess, the hip young couple never spoke to me again. But then they were smug trendoid architects who only bought in our neighborhood because it was cheap. We didn't interest them, and neither did any of their other neighbors.

I tried to invite them over for coffee after this episode. They were so taken aback, it was as if I'd invited them to come with me to scavenge a landfill. "What? Um... no, sorry, we're busy. Forever."

In any event, that episode ended any real attempts I made to actually nap while I was alone with my children. Instead, I'd wait until they were invited to a birthday party, drop them off and run home and climb into bed. Alone. Just to sleep.

Eventually, the hostess would call and inquire if I ever intended to pick up my kids.

"I'll have to think about it," I was always tempted to reply.

## NO, OFFICER, THAT'S NOT MY CHILD

WHEN YOU become a parent, you hear horrifying things come out of your mouth, such as, "Just wait until you have children of your own!"

This is likely to send you into a major depression, because you never dreamed you'd utter such terrible clichés.

And you never thought you could possibly be as bad a parent as yours were. I assure you, though, this is normal, so relax and don't grab the Prozac—unless you're going to share with the rest of us.

I don't have any drugs for you, but I do have one phrase to use when your kids are driving up your blood pressure to the point that you feel you might actually have a stroke any second. I invented this phrase, and I can vouch for its calming effect. Seriously, give it a try. I'll offer you a money-back guarantee. Are you ready? Here's the phrase:

"That's not my child."

This phrase is very calming whenever your kid is embarrassing you. Maybe in your heart you know it's not true, but still keep uttering it as a mantra. It will help keep the red from your cheeks and the mortification at bay.

I used it for the first time many years ago, when I took my kids to an art museum. At some point, after cackling loudly and freaking out the guards by trying to touch every painting, they decided to crawl on their hands and knees through the galleries, pretending to be kitty cats. My hissed exhortations to "Get up! Get up now!" were met only by emphatic "Meows."

Finally, I just ordered them to follow me and walked out of the museum, uttering this mantra to myself. They crawled and meowed until we got to the car, and I lived to face another day.

The phrase was also useful when we faced another artwork, this one an immense replica of Michelangelo's "David," which dominated the shopping arcade at Caesars Palace in Las Vegas. Since this nude statue is about 8,000 feet high, or so it seemed at the time, his fig leaf is about eighty feet high.

Confronted with a colossal naked marble man, the kids pointed and started squealing, "He's naked!"

Except that those words echoed in the marble halls, so it actually sounded like "HEEEEEE"S NAAAAKKK-KKEEEED," as the sound reverberated around the entire center and its overpriced designer boutiques. I just walked away, red-faced, and murmured to myself, "They're not my kids. They're not my kids. I never saw those kids before in my entire life."

On another occasion in Nevada, I had just taken the kids to a buffet where they got ice cream cones, and we were walking through a casino while I decided whether it was worth writing a travel story or not.

Out of the corner of my eye, I became vaguely aware that the kids were doing something odd as they trailed along behind me. But as soon as I would turn around, they would look angelic and take a lick from their cones.

Then a casino security guard came up to me and said gruffly, "Ma'am, please make your children stop licking the mirrors."

For reasons known only to God, the kids were taking licks of their ice cream, and then licking every mirrored column we passed in the casino.

"Sorry," I told the guard. "Those aren't my children." And I walked away.

Well, I didn't really say that, but I wanted to.

Next week's calming phrase: It's not my problem.

## MY KIDS HAVE A DREADED DISEASE

IT'S SAD when you have to admit that your children have a disease, and even sadder when you can't seem to find a cure. Even though this disease is very common, I have yet to see a telethon, a 5K run-walk, a hospital wing, or even a magnetic bumper sticker in support of its sufferers.

This disease is called Closeophobia, and I'm sorry to say my children are both sufferers.

Closeophobia, also known in psychiatric lingo as Shutophobia, is the fear of closing anything they have previously opened. This disease can be transmitted to anything that the sufferers have touched. Commonly affected items:

- Kitchen drawers
- Kitchen cabinets
- Bread wrappers
- Cereal boxes
- Milk jugs
- Bedroom drawers
- Closet doors
- Refrigerator doors
- Front doors
- Back doors
- Screen doors
- Bathroom cabinets
- Rear hatch doors
- CD players

It does not appear to be contagious, but unfortunately scientists have not been able to find a cure or perfect a vaccine. My doctor said there's not even a medication for the sufferer that's effective without serious side effects, though Valium or Prozac may be effective for the rest of the immediate family.

Applied properly, duct tape can work, but it's not practical as a long-term fix.

There have been cases reported that have been cured by alert and especially skillful parenting, but I've never observed this myself, so I can't give any advice.

In our house, Cheetah Boy has the worst case. He can leave a trail of destruction through our house that's worthy of a FEMA grant. And things seem to have become worse since he became a teenager this year.

One useful aspect to this affliction is that I always know where Cheetah Boy has been immediately before the outbreak. For example, I know when my son has raided my sock drawer, because it's left open, with miscellaneous knitted footwear draped over the front.

Curly Girl has a better time of it, though she tends to have outbreaks on mornings when she's trying to hurry to school.

They haven't located the exact spot on the gene sequence where this hereditary disease is located, but it appears to be related to Spacecadetitis, the same illness that causes kids to leave wet towels strewn around the house and throw cutlery in the trash.

While they don't have a cure, I have come up with several stress management techniques for parents that I use around my own house, to greater or lesser effect:

Shouting, "Were you born in a barn? Come and close this right now!"

Waking the sufferer up in the middle of the night to put away food left open at bedtime.

Refusing to leave the house for events until all containers have been closed.

To mitigate the effect of the symptoms on a parent, I advise one glass of red wine, taken as needed. A shot of tequila can be substituted as necessary.

## THE HORRIBLE CURSE
## OF THE SCIENCE PROJECT

IT'S TRUE! It's alive! And coming to a school near you. That's right. It's time for the dreaded science project to emerge like the undead from its grave.

Once a year, I have a panic attack at my kids' school, also known as the science project.

I realize there are parents who like helping their kids with the science fair. But they are either scientists themselves or certifiably insane.

Other parents in the known galaxy look on this season with fear and loathing. Because, as we all know, the project's success has little to do with the child and almost everything to do with how much effort and money the parent is willing to pour into it, while the kids are in the next room playing video games.

Why can't the kids ever do a Mom-approved science project? I would be perfectly happy to help them with any of these:

- How does the temperature of the hot water change in the house before and after you wash all the dishes?
- What types of mold are living on the P.E. uniforms at the bottom of the laundry hamper? Does washing remove them?
- Who can take out the trash faster? A male child or a female child?
- What is the effect of scouring powder on the bacteria in the bottom of our sink?
- What actually lies at the bottom of the floor in the back seat of the car, buried under the layers of kid junk? Come to think of it, that might be more like an archaeology project.

This year, I have two kids doing projects. I tried to get Curly Girl to write a report on rocks and minerals. I even offered to spend a whole $8.95 on a "geology field trip in a bag." But she insists on doing a project instead. She's going to measure which dog biscuits dogs like best. That, at least, is easy to understand. And, since it involves dogs, I won't have to pester her to work on it.

Cheetah Boy, however, decided he wanted to make an "earthquake-resistant building" for his project this year. Don't you think that sounds easy, like you could probably find instructions online and glue a couple of egg cartons and straws together? Even I could handle that. But, of course, it's deceptively hard. After hours of online searching, we have yet to find instructions for how to build one of the freaking things.

While I was frantically Googling this afternoon, on my day off, after taking pity on my son's frustrated trying, all I could think of was, "I could be sitting back with my feet up for a few minutes of leisure right now, the first I've had all day long. Instead, I'm at the computer, trying to find a design for some lame device that means nothing in the real world."

Cheetah Boy has many talents, but the odds of him becoming a seismic engineer, I would say realistically, are slim to none.

One thing to be grateful for: The manufactured monster that is the school science fair lurches into our lives only once a year.

## SUMMER CAMP STRESS

IT'S SUMMER camp season, the time of year when you magically forget the 10,006 things your kids did to annoy you the day before they left, and focus only on the fact that they have gone to sleep-away camp and left you behind.

By coincidence, both of my rugrats are gone at the same time. Curly Girl went to Camp Fire camp in the mountains, and Cheetah Boy to Boy Scout camp on Fiesta Island in San Diego's Mission Bay. Since I didn't make any plans to party hearty this week, there's a lot of moping going on around here, both by me and the dog, in a house that is both eerily quiet and freakishly clean.

I opened the desk drawer this morning, and there were the scissors, right where I left them. That alone would have told me that something was awry.

I walked into the bathroom, and the towels were hung up, instead of lying on the floor in a wet heap.

My front lawn looks like respectable people live here, instead of hillbillies who litter it every day with toys, baseball bats, scooters, skateboards, and candy wrappers.

No one is bickering over, well, anything.

It's like being in an episode of *The Twilight Zone*.

This year is different, since people have fully embraced the power of the Web to provide kid-sick parents with visual images of their offspring, if not the real thing. My daughter's Camp Fire leader posted pictures of the girls getting off the bus and eating lunch up at camp, only hours after they left. I felt a little teary looking at Curly Girl having fun without me. Cheetah Boy's leaders also put up a slide show, and I greedily looked for him in every shot. He looks happy and not too sunburned, in his dream beach campsite right on the bay.

It's hard to realize your kids can do just fine without you, and that you can't do the same without them.

I'll have to do this again, when they both head off to church camp in the mountains. Maybe then I'll be better organized, and have something fun to do myself. Anyone got any lanyards or wood to carve? Maybe some chocolate and marshmallows to make s'mores in the backyard . . .?

## PARKING-LOT SITTING FOR FUN

BEFORE I had kids, I couldn't imagine spending hours and

hours each week sitting in a series of parking lots, unless it was accompanied by a grill, a portable blender, and a crowd of friends waiting for the big game to start.

But this is one of the many surprises that parenthood springs on you, especially when you forgot to get the parenting manual, as I did. I don't imagine moms in Manhattan are sitting around in SUVs waiting for Junior to finish his lesson, but the parking lot syndrome is a well-established fact of suburban life.

This doesn't become evident right away because in the beginning, the little angels are so tiny that they need your help even to blow their noses. You're always on call, like the ICU nurse, twenty-four hours per day, seven days a week.

By the time the kidlets are old enough to study piano, join a team, run around a base or pick flowers in the outfield, however, they're being supervised for an hour by someone who's not you. This gives you a chance to dart out to the grocery store and get milk. Hooray.

However, I'm always stressed out, because I fear that the errand will take too long, and the practice will be over, and my child will be standing there with the coach, humiliated, eyes casting daggers at you, after everyone else is gone.

The opportunity to run errands unaccompanied by small, noisy anchors is always worth taking. But at a certain point, you may, like me, decide that you'd rather preserve your sanity than have fresh bread in the house. What the heck, you can always toast it. They won't know the difference.

That's when you start camping out in your car instead of racing around on a frantic errand. Not only does this mean less stress in your life, but it may be the only time—ever—you get to be alone.

If you've had children, you know they are deeply insulted when you try to conduct a phone conversation with anyone within their hearing. They will start asking you moronic, pointless questions, and won't stop until you finally hang up in frustration. Then, they'll turn and walk away, having achieved their purpose.

It's the same with any stolen attempts to read a book. The busiest, most otherwise occupied child will come to a complete halt when he sees you reading a book and devote the next half-hour of his young life to making sure you never get off page 221. Sandwiches and juice boxes must be immediately procured, shoes must be hunted down. It doesn't matter what excuse is given; the objective is to keep you from reading your book.

That's what's so surprising and fine about the parking lot situation. The first few times you're stuck in a parking lot, waiting for your kid to emerge from soccer practice or tutoring, you're slightly annoyed. After all, parking lots are generally not landscaped. They tend to be gray and ugly hunks of tarmac. There's seldom any beauty to be contemplated.

But after a while, you realize that for this stolen hour, this brief period, no one is yelling at you to kill the spider under her bed. There's no homework to be located. No counters to be wiped. There's just you and the car and the book you brought with you, or maybe the phone on which you plan to have your first uninterrupted conversation in five years.

When I used to drop my kids off at softball and baseball practice, at the same park, I always saw parents sitting and watching their kids. I did feel guilty that I wasn't Supermom, not only attending their games but every practice as well.

Then, I went back to my car and started plowing through the latest thriller.

Nowadays, my kids are much older and they give me plenty of time by myself, especially on the weekends. Still, I find that I enjoy that quiet time in the car, when the teens are at tutoring or volunteering at church. Sometimes my heart sinks when someone walks up to talk to me. I roll the window down with dismay.

Too soon, I fear I won't have any reason to sit in a parking lot at all, because the teens will be gone and far away. Then, I guess I'll have to go back to tailgating again . . .

## WHY DO KIDS REFUSE TO WEAR WARM CLOTHES?

I DON'T know if it's unique to kids in Southern California, who hardly ever face any real weather, but every time it's nasty outside, I have such a battle with my kids to dress appropriately for school.

Once a cold storm from Alaska pelted us with frigid rain. In what he considered to be an appropriate response, Cheetah Boy, then age twelve, came out of his room dressed for school in a T-shirt and shorts.

I pointed out to him that this isn't the Bahamas; it was freezing outside, and he needed to wear long pants.

"Mom, I don't have any long pants," he insisted with a bit of a snarl, which means they're all buried at the bottom of his closet (an area that hasn't been excavated since the museum ran out of money), so he can't find them and doesn't want to wear them anyway.

"You will wear long pants to school today or be grounded when you get home," I told him. I reminded him that, only last night, he refused to wear a sweater to our church concert and shivered the entire night.

I mean, it wasn't like I was asking him to wear a fur-lined parka, hunt baby seals, and eat blubber. I just wanted to know he was warm. The kid has no meat on him whatsoever. He's always cold.

Fortunately, he decided to find some long pants and put them on, but then he wanted to walk to school in a thin

sweatshirt that would have been soaking wet in two minutes. Amazingly enough, we only had a short battle before
he agreed to wear a rain poncho, but no amount of remon-
stration would get him to change out his thin Vans canvas
sneakers for appropriate footwear. Fashion has no common
sense, as anyone can see when they walk past a woman crip-
pled by high heels.

When I adopted my kids, I read a great book called
*Parenting With Love and Logic,* by Foster Cline MD and
Jim Fay, about allowing your kids to learn responsibility by
making their own choices, and then having to live with the
consequences. Like, refuse to dress warmly and be chilled
all day, with the idea that, next time, they'll know better. In
general, I've tried to follow its precepts and have been very
happy with the results.

But I also subscribe to the "enough is enough" theory,
which says that sometimes, like during storms from Alaska,
kids just have to do what they're told. In the past, they've
come home shivering and soaking wet, and that's just not
okay with me.

Unlike her brother, on that rainy day Curly Girl decided
on her own to wear warm leggings under her skirt (it goes
without saying that she's not putting on a pair of pants). But
then we battled for half an hour over what she was wearing
on top. Three times she came out in some sweater one might
wear to a tea party on the Equator in July. Three times, I
sent her back to change. By the end of this, she was late for
school and we were both really crabby.

Eventually, she put on a waterproof parka, but only after
an epic battle they could have filmed for the next *Lord of the
Rings.* The reason for this mystifies me.

Is it just that it rains in Southern California so seldom,
the kids are driven mad by it? Do they consider warm clothing some sort of terrible punishment devised by parents to

torture them?

I once had a cat, Bob, who was born at the beginning of our last severe drought. For four years, the cat never saw rain. Then, finally, it started raining hard. Bob became demented and kept running around the house, meowing at the top of his lungs, demanding that I do something to stop it.

"Sorry, Bob," I told him. "There's nothing I can do."

Maybe the weather drives my kids crazy like that, too.


## FORCE-FEEDING CULTURE

I TOOK my kids to an art museum on Presidents Day even though Cheetah Boy had made it clear he'd rather spend his holiday getting a root canal. My son's recalcitrance caused me some concern, because I could only see a Smithsonian-sized hunk of misery in my future if I forced him to come against his will.

See, Cheetah Boy's idea of fun does not involve even one of the Great Masterpieces of World Art. His notion of fun is to hit 837 tennis balls in the front yard with his big-barrel bat, trying to dent as many neighbors' cars as possible. (Just kidding; he's not really trying to damage them. I think.) When he tires of that, he likes to lie on the couch watching the same *iCarly* episode thirty-six times in a row.

However, if I left him at home, and just went to the museum with Curly Girl, I couldn't help wondering if I would be depriving him of a worthwhile experience.

A 2006 study by Harvard researchers found, believe it or not, that the only activity outside of school that seemed to be a factor in whether high school students get into elite universities is visits to art museums. But (and pay attention here) the students don't have to visit the art museums themselves—the correlation was only whether their parents visit art museums.

So I'm sure Cheetah Boy would argue that he could stay home and watch *iCarly* while I go to the art museum on the quest to get him into Harvard.

Since I didn't bother to share this argument with him, I decided to take him anyway, and just used plain old bribery: If the two kids found certain paintings that I chose for a scavenger hunt, then they could have a double scoop of ice cream on the way home.

Since my kids would climb Mount Everest barefoot for ice cream, this did the trick.

When we got to the Los Angeles County Museum of Art, I discovered greatly to my pleasure that they have a new program called NexGen that provides free admission all the time to kids and one adult per child.

The kids got special tags to wear around their necks, and we also got a family guide to the museum with color photos of some of the exhibits.

I promptly assigned Cheetah Boy a David Hockney painting as his first scavenger item to find. He took the photo to a guard, and quickly found its location at the front of a gallery. Then, he turned around and started speed walking toward the exit.

"Hey, where are you going?" I asked him, before he could disappear down the stairs.

"I'm done," he answered. "You told me to find it and I found it. Now, let's get ice cream."

I explained, greatly to his chagrin, that he now had to actually look at some of the paintings in the gallery before he got any frozen sugary treats. I'm not sure he looked at any art, but he did throw his stuffed animal up and down 387 times quietly, so at least his sister and I could walk around and admire the many Great Masterpieces uninterrupted.

We spent a few hours looking, and, as usual, got worn

out before we'd seen all the collections. On the way home, we stopped at Rite Aid so the kids could get their double scoops, though once again they were out of mint chocolate chip.

If you work at Rite Aid, can you explain why they are always, always out of mint chocolate chip? You'd think if it were so popular, they'd keep more on hand.

And I think I can now use the threat of the art museum to get Cheetah Boy to agree to almost anything.

"Get that room clean, please, or we're going to the art museum."

"Finish your homework, or we're going to the art museum."

## WE'RE VIDEO GAME–FREE, DULL, AND STAYING THAT WAY

WE HAVE the only house in our neighborhood with no video games. My son has explained to me many times how this makes us freakish aliens from space.

I truly believe that video games were created by Satan to turn otherwise normal children into his drooling, glassy-eyed stooges. After my son plays them at his friends' houses, he comes home irritable and testy for the rest of the day. Even though his skin is normally mocha-colored, after a day spent in a darkened room with a controller in his hand, he comes home with a sickly pallor.

This is a huge dilemma for me, because I always had this fantasy that my house would be the one that all the kids congregated at after school. I would be the "fun mom," the one who made frozen pops, the one in the TV commercial with all the kids crowded around the kitchen counter, demanding more of those little pizza nuggets.

Unfortunately, since we have neither video games nor

a swimming pool, this does not happen. No one demands over-processed Kraft snack foods from my kitchen—because my son goes over to other kids' houses to get his video fix.

And it seems, where we live at least, that middle school boys can't do anything in packs except play video games. So without them, these boys inhabit our house for only nano-seconds before they want to leave.

This dilemma led me this Christmas to consider getting a video game system, at least a Wii that we could all play together. The kids pointed out that I spent $82 the last time we all went bowling, and with the Wii, we could bowl at home for free.

But with other priorities like a new bike and sewing machine, no Wii got purchased. Plus, Cheetah Boy got a C on his report card, and I don't want to reward him with anything until that grade comes up.

My anti-video game attitude was only reinforced recently when I read a story in the Boston Herald about a mom who was so frustrated by her son's obsessive video gaming that she finally called 911.

Apparently, her fourteen-year-old had become so fixated on *Grand Theft Auto* that he refused to stop playing it. The trouble in her house started after she woke up at 2 a.m. and found her son playing the game on his bedroom computer. In case you're not familiar with *Grand Theft Auto*, this is a socially conscious educational game in which players portray criminals and earn points by stealing cars, killing people and destroying property.

This mom unplugged her son's computer when he refused to get off, which led to a fight, which led to a visit from the cops. It took two Boston cops to persuade the kid to turn off his video game and go to bed.

Somehow, that doesn't surprise me one bit. I see kids walking around, oblivious to the world, with those hand-held video games everywhere I go.

We have family friends whose son has a game he's allowed to play only in the car. Often, when they come over, he pesters his mom over and over to go out to the car, because apparently there's not enough fun to be had in our house without this boy and my son sitting in the car playing the thing.

Here's my question: When do kids ever think these days? When do they ever have brains free from electronics long enough to ponder the universe? To think of things that might someday lead them to a cure for cancer?

If Sir Isaac Newton had been playing a video game, I'm sure he never would have noticed the apple falling from the tree, so he never would have formulated the theory of gravity.

I was an odd, geeky kid most of my childhood. I was too weird for most of the other kids to play with, so I spent most of my time reading obsessively, which of course only made me more of a dweeb. The difference is, in all that reading, I was actually learning stuff about the world, in a way that kids today never will.

I was also learning to think creatively, spell and build my vocabulary to the point that I was able to get a job as a professional writer, where people pay me to ride on fire engines, go on ride-alongs with cops and insult the makers of video games.

My kids do play games, outdoors in the fresh air, where they're building their muscles and hopefully a lifetime habit of fitness. What are the kids who play *Grand Theft Auto* learning? How to be carjackers? How to be pursued by police? Those are skills I really want my children to acquire. Maybe we can get the entire *Grand Theft Auto* series and start a new crime-family dynasty.

## THE MAD HOLIDAY DASH

IT'S CHRISTMAS season again. So far, I've done about one nanosecond of all the things I need to get done. If this were a marathon, I would have finished the first 10 feet, before stopping to pant and look around for cookies.

The biggest unfinished project or chore, depending on your outlook, is the ritual purchase of the tree.

I have grudgingly decided to get a real tree this year, after a comment from a faithful reader that was too true: My kids soon will be grown and won't care a whit what I do, because they'll be lying on the beach in Hawaii with their spouses for Christmas while I'll be sitting at home with the dog, watching the pope give midnight Mass in Rome.

So I guess I'll give them what they want now, while they actually care, and then when they're blowing off Dear Old Mom at Christmas to go to the Caribbean, I can get a fake one. Or maybe head to the Bahamas myself.

I'm hoping the rain will hold off long enough for me to make the trek to the cheap Christmas tree lot. I'm planning to give my kids some Prozac so they won't bicker for an hour over which of nine hundred eighty-six identical trees to pick.

It's already becoming clear there will be no nicely wrapped plates of Christmas cookies delivered to the neighbors this year, at least none emanating from our house. I actually never do this, you understand, but I always feel guilty that I don't. One year, I bought adorable holiday cookie cutters, but after we made the cookies, we ate them all the same day. Then the cookie cutters got put away, never to be seen again. If you find them, let me know.

Then there's the gift list to finish. Shopping for teens and tweens isn't as much fun as when they were little, when you got to satisfy your own inner child. One of the best things about having kids is that you get to relive your own childhood and make it come out the way you wanted back then.

You didn't get a life-size, robotic stuffed pony when you were little, but you can give one to your kid now. You didn't get a giant Barbie dream house with real lights and an actual swimming pool, but your precious princess can get one now, thanks to slave labor in China.

The problem with shopping for older kids is that nothing they want was even invented when I was their age. There were no iPods or video games, no cell phones, no digital cameras, basically nothing that kids want these days. This makes my own personal wish fulfillment for my teens harder to come by.

And it is all about me, after all.

At least they had bicycles and scooters, so you might be able to guess what Santa is bringing to our house this year.

I have this quixotic goal of actually mailing my presents to loved ones far away before I have to pay for two-day air freight. Every year, this is my Impossible Dream. And every year, I end up shelling out as much for shipping as I do for the gifts themselves.

My brother has just given up and started sending us all gift cards, which the kids love because they get to pick out their own presents. I do like getting gift cards, but I'm still firmly in the camp of sending real gifts, though at some point I might just abandon that and join the club.

Since I became a single mom, I have abandoned all the craft projects I used to do this time of year. Now it's just a race to complete a set of necessary tasks by December twenty-fifth, and try to have some fun along the way.

The craziest day is always Christmas Eve, don't you think? Usually, I work all day, then madly wrap a few remaining gifts, bellow at the kids to hurry up and get ready, dash over to the church for the annual Christmas pageant and service, get home and fix dinner, bake cookies for Santa and put some carrots out for his reindeer, make the kids go to bed and then wait for them to go to sleep, before Santa can come and put out all their presents under the tree.

Santa doesn't wrap the presents he leaves for them. Curly Girl asked about this one year, but I explained that Santa gets tired.

I enjoy crawling into my bed on Christmas Eve, and I even like being awakened three hours later by kids who want to inform me that Santa has come, though I make them go back to bed until six in the morning. When I was a child, my younger brother would always make me go in to wake up our parents, on the theory that our dad was less likely to whack me than him.

I've been warned by friends that this will be over soon, that teenagers sleep in on Christmas morning. That hasn't happened yet, but I don't know whether it will be good or bad.

## MY DAUGHTER DOESN'T NEED ANY MAKEUP, THANK YOU

I DID a double-take when I looked at my daughter the other day, because her eyes looked funny.

They seemed to have something strange around them. It even looked like . . .

Yikes . . . it was eyeliner!

Somehow, my tiny baby girl had sneaked eyeliner into her daily routine, and I had completely failed to notice. I realized immediately that her eyelids had been looking darker for a while now, and I had only taken this fact in on a subliminal level. Sort of like how people refuse to acknowledge their spouse is cheating when he hasn't come home for three days, or that the dog has a problem when your couch reeks of urine.

Curly Girl just turned twelve, and I admit I shouldn't have freaked out that she smuggled my ancient eyeliner pencil out of its case and started using it, after wiping off the layers of dust.

After all, many girls are starting to smear goop on their faces at about that age. I did it, too, and even more scarily, in those days white lipstick was the big thing, apparently in the belief that corpses are attractive.

But honestly, she's so pretty that I just can't see any reason why she needs to wear makeup, other than a little lip gloss.

I have no moral objection to makeup. I don't think it's intrinsically sinful. Once a year, I even put on a little lipstick to go out to dinner. Or I used to, before my one lipstick mysteriously disappeared from my makeup bag. At the time, I thought it was mice. Now, I'm not so sure.

When I was younger, I was a slave to the cosmetics industry. I spent hundreds of dollars a year on products to wipe, swipe, brush, slather, sponge, and curl all over my face, in the mistaken impression that this made me look better. But as time went on, I realized that I was happy with myself in my natural state, without any goo that made my face break out or mascara that gave me raccoon eyes.

This was heightened when I went camping at a park in Malibu. I went into the bathroom in the morning to discover that it was full of, and I'm serious here, teenage girls who were carefully applying thick layers of makeup, apparently so they would look better to the squirrels and seagulls on their hikes.

At that time, I vowed that any daughter I had would not fall victim to the rich and powerful international cosmetics industry conspiracy, which exists solely to convince women that they don't ever look okay, even naked in the shower.

This was made easier by the fact that Curly Girl is naturally pretty, which I feel I can say without bragging since she has none of my DNA whatsoever. I don't think it's wrong for girls to wear makeup if they need it to hide flaws or acne, as long as they realize that less is more and that blue eye shadow was invented for the sole purpose of making young girls look like hookers working Hollywood Boulevard. However, for a pretty girl like my daughter, who at least for now has a beautiful complexion, to be putting stuff on her face is just gilding the lily.

I know a lot of men agree. Surveys show that men prefer their women without makeup.

You'll never read this, though, in a fashion magazine, which gets a huge chunk of its advertising revenue from companies seeking to induce you to buy, buy, buy that latest product that will turn you into a goddess.

We don't have any of these magazines in our house, and we never will. Along with high heels, long fingernails, and tight skirts, makeup is one of those things women are taught to favor, even though it's expensive, unnecessary, and, in some cases, bad for them.

And, Curly Girl, can you give me back my lipstick? I might need it one of these days.

# 2

# WHO WANTS
# MY PARENTING
# ADVICE?

## THE PROS AND CONS
## OF BEING AN OLD-BROAD MOM

SO DEMI Moore adopted a baby at age forty-six. And, no, that's not too old.

When she made the leap to adopt, I had an immediate flashback to my own forty-sixth year, when a lot of people—even my own mother—thought I was a few fries short of a Happy Meal for adopting two kids as a working single mom. Cheetah Boy and Curly Girl were five and three at the time, and came to me through the L.A. County foster system.

It was easily the most thrilling and terrifying thing I've ever done.

Meanwhile, my friends who weren't parents were dining out at a lot of nice places and had become financially comfortable, but they might as well have been crocheting lace doilies, because they were starting to act like fussy old ladies.

"Can you make your kids go in the other room, dear?" a dear friend who's my exact age tells me in a voice that's recently started to sound creaky and aged. "They are making an awful racket."

Well, no, I can't, because I enjoy hearing the sound of my children play. Plus, I have already learned that too-quiet children are objects of suspicion.

That's only one of the transformations that takes place when you become an old-broad mom. You are forced, sometimes against your will, to be in touch with pop culture.

Imagine this: I didn't even know who SpongeBob SquarePants was before my kids moved in six years ago. And I probably would have gone my entire life without watching a single *High School Musical* movie. Imagine the shame.

A study found that new moms in their forties were the happiest of all mothers, because they'd already been out there and done it all, and they were happy to settle down with their munchkins, who seemed at that point in their lives like gifts from heaven. Here are some pros and cons of being a creaky old mom:

**The downside**

- You are always the oldest mom in any group. Sometimes people think you're Grandma.
- You might not be around to see your grandkids grow up.
- You have to go to a lot of events involving bad pizza.
- It takes more energy than you think possible to chase them around.
- The financial burden of parenting is a horrible shock to a mom who's used to traveling, eating well, and buying double lattes at Starbucks.
- You have to plan for college tuition and retirement at the same time.
- Your own parents are too old to help out much.
- You go from having every minute to yourself to never having one second to yourself.
- You have to trade your cool sports car for a Mommymobile.
- Your kids harass you when you dye the gray out of your hair.
- Your hormones will make you crazy while you go through menopause, exactly when your kids' hormones are going crazy in the other direction.
- You could face a major health crisis while your kids are still at home.
- You will someday have to enter a Chuck E. Cheese restaurant.

**The upside**

- You are more likely to be financially stable.
- You're not nearly as stupid as you were in your twenties.

- You've already been to every bar and heard every pick-up line, so dating is less important.
- You can't get old because your kids need you to have a youthful attitude.
- Sitting at freezing-cold baseball and soccer games preserves your body.
- You can finally declare "head of household" on your income taxes.
- Your life acquires a level of meaning you didn't even know existed: i.e., to keep your kids alive until they grow up and marry someone you don't like.
- You get to relive your own childhood and make it come out the way you wanted. Hey, kids, let's go to Disneyland! Let's learn to play the guitar. Let's build a four-foot-high dollhouse.
- Kids have more love to share than you ever imagined possible.

And, the most important reason: The joy of coming home to a child running toward you with open arms, shouting, "Mommy! Mommy! Mommy! Finally, you're home!" is beyond words to describe.

## SCHOOL'S STARTING AGAIN. THANK GOD.

SURE, in the summer it's great to get to sleep in and not have to rush my kids off in the morning. But all good things must come to an end, and besides, there's lots to look forward to when they go back to school. Like the first day of back to class. Always so exciting. My kids even comb their hair. Voluntarily.

After they leave I can clean the house and it will stay tidy for entire hours, instead of nanoseconds. I can actually have peace while I'm working at home, instead of listening to this scintillating, David Mamet-like dialogue: "You shut up." "No, you shut up." "I told you to shut up first."

No one will stomp into the kitchen every seven minutes yelling, "I'm hungry, what have we got to eat?" and then reject every culinary classic that I offer.

And maybe this year the kids will go back to music class and actually learn to play their instruments better, instead of just torturing them. And me. And the dog. And the neighbors.

The adorable offspring won't be pestering me 846 times a day with their favorite six-word phrase: "I'm bored, can I watch TV?" I won't feel guilty for relenting and letting them watch TV, just so they'll be quiet and let me work.

They'll bring home so many fun things to do, like science projects and dioramas that are due in twelve hours.

I will have fewer opportunities to feel inadequate because I'm not the "cool mom" with the pool and deluxe video game at her house.

And finally, those two words: Early. Bedtime.

## THE UPSIDE
## TO BEING A SINGLE MOM

IT'S HARD but rewarding to be a single mom. I wish my adopted children had an adoptive father as well as a mother, but, sadly, they don't.

So I try to look on the bright side, like remembering the day when someone came up to me at work, looking like she'd been up all night, and whispered in my ear, "You're lucky to be single. You don't have to fight with your husband over the kids." So I count the blessings of singledom, including:

1. There's no one to say "I told you so" when you make a horrible parenting mistake, which I do at least once a day.

2. I might not have the earning power of a two-income couple, but at least no one is telling me how to spend the money I do have.
3. I call the shots. Putting the kids into private school or deciding whether to hold Junior back a year in kindergarten. You decide.
4. The kids can't divide and conquer. There's only one of me, so when I say no, there's no one to appeal to.
5. You can lavish all your energy on the children, at least the energy that's left after work. You don't have to worry about making a spouse happy, too.

## YOU CALL THAT PARENTING ADVICE?

OSCAR Wilde said the only thing to do with good advice is to pass it on, because it's never of any use to oneself.

And it always amazes me how many people want to give me parenting advice, especially those who never have raised any children themselves. In fact, have you noticed that people with no kids often seem to know more about child-rearing than you do?

Please don't take this the wrong way, but if no one has ever spit up on your silk shirt just as you were walking out the door, required you to change the bed sheets at two o'clock in the morning or embarrassed you in a grocery store, I'm not going to give your advice much credence.

And if you're Dr. Laura, and you didn't know your own mother had passed away and was finally found two months later in her condo, I'm not going to be taking advice from you, either.

And if you're a magazine writer, I'm probably not going to be using your extremely complicated methods for improving my parenting, though I might tear out the pages and make paper airplanes out of them.

Apparently I'm not the only one. Readers over the years have shared with me the wrong, awkward and just plain stupid advice they've received. I really like when they tell me how messed up their own kids are, because then I can relax and think that maybe I'm not doing things completely wrong after all. And, really, sometimes it seems incredible that kids actually made it to adulthood.

Take a look at some of the actual parenting advice floating around out there:

"Add white sugar to my newborns' water so they would like the taste and drink it."

"My mom told me not to hug my kids too much."

"Give in to your kids, no matter what, so that they know you love them."

"Don't breast feed. It's just too much trouble!"

"When a baby is teething, rub whiskey on their gums."

"If you pick them up too much, they are going to be spoiled."

"Children should be seen and not heard."

"When my mom realized my oldest is left-handed, she ordered me to tie his left hand behind his back so that he could live in a right-handed world."

Come to think of it, maybe parents aren't the best sources of advice . . .

## DIGGING FOR THE TRUTH

ALL RIGHT, so the kid just told me a big, fat lie. What do I do about this?

Have a long, earnest talk with him about the importance of honesty? Smack his rear end with the flyswatter? Ground him from video games for a week? Call Jimmy Swaggart?

If you're hoping I have an answer here, then you are sadly mistaken. Because I have no bleeping idea.

One of the vexing things about parenthood is that half the time, I really have no idea what I'm doing. I just ricochet from one thing to another, like a pinball in an arcade. And, just when I think I've found a solution, the kids change the problem.

This is when it's harder to be a single mom. You are the sole custodian of these miniature human beings, responsible for their character and moral development, even when you secretly know you can't be trusted to keep a goldfish alive.

Thinking a male influence might help in this situation, I asked my friend Norberto what to do when Cheetah Boy misbehaved.

"Make him dig holes," Norberto said.

Evidently when Norberto's dad, who was a Cuban refugee, wanted to dole out punishment he made Noberto and his brothers dig holes in the yard. Now, this appealed to me in several ways, not the least of which was it would get my human perpetual motion machine, otherwise known as Cheetah Boy, tired out. But having seen the movie "Holes," I can't really see myself as an evil prison warden, even if it is as Sigourney Weaver.

Plus, my backyard is a concrete patio.

My mom used to beat the back of my legs with a switch and my dad threatened us with a belt, although he never actually hit me, that I recall, though he walloped my brother plenty. I watched all those TV shows like Andy Griffith as a child, where the parent has the Deep Earnest Talk with the child and permanently changes his behavior, as demonstrated by the next scene where the kid gives back the bike, or confesses he copied his homework.

But I guess I don't have the right spiel, because my kids blow straight through the Deep Earnest Talk, ask me if I'm done yet and, by the way, what's for dinner?

Some days, I just wish kids were like accounting. You get a calculator and a set of books and if you stay at it long enough, the numbers add up.

Instead, they're more like fish. Slippery, beautiful, mysterious, in their own world and sometimes quite smelly.

## WRECK-IT RALPH, MOVE OVER

HELLO and welcome to my parental support group. This week's topic: kids who wreck stuff.

Before I had kids, I used to feel vaguely slighted that my friends with children only wanted to hang out with others of their own kind. Now I know why.

Childfree people have sparkling houses that look like TV commercials—after the Merry Maids have been there. They have Ming vases and family heirlooms on their fireplace mantles, which have never, even once, been used as a backboard for bouncing tennis balls.

They have appliances that have never been dismantled by anyone without a factory license.

Childless people have never called a plumber to extract decapitated Barbie heads from the toilet. My plumber recently told me he's looking for beachfront property, and all I could think was, "Yeah, with money I've paid you in the past eight years."

If a genie appeared and I could magically become any character on the TV show *Desperate Housewives*, I would definitely want to be Susan, because she's married to a plumber. That would save me at least $845,222 a year that I now pay to extract nickels from the garbage disposal, remove toothpaste caps from the drainpipe ... well, I could go on, but then I'd have to go lie down.

Right now, I'm looking over at a couch that sags in the back. It looks a little sad, because a very boisterous boy jumped on it and gave it a permanent herniated disk.

As part of my parenting support mission, in which misery is shared, I asked readers on my Facebook fan page to tell me about some things their kids ruined, and they didn't let me down. I offered a copy of the book *Sh*t My Kids Ruined* for the best anecdote, and loyal reader April was the winner. As you read this, note how April throws her husband under the bus, as all clever wives do:

April: "We were visiting England and staying at a friend of my husband's parents' house. I managed to keep my two-year-old under control in the beautifully decorated house, full of small breakables. On the last night, my daughter wanted to keep looking at books with the light on. My husband said, 'She is on vacation, too. Let her keep the light on.' A few hours later I went to check on her, and she had found a small red marker and drawn about a ten-foot mural above the bed, all around it! While I myself am an art lover, yellow paint and red marker do not mix! We tried everything to get it clean, and it would not come off.

"The people were out of town, so we left a big bottle of booze with a note, 'Please drink this before going upstairs.' Being the wonderful British people that they were, they called and said they were so sorry that we must have felt so bad! I call this the International Incident. My daughter is thirteen now, and a bit less destructive, but it took three coats of paint to cover that wall, and several years later a guest was sleeping in that room and noticed a red line going around the inside of the lamp shade above the bed—just a friendly reminder of the bad American two-year-old."

And here's one sent in by a reader named Cindy: "My son, then twelve, wanted to know how a microwave 'really' worked. So he took it apart, piece by piece, and made pictures and labels (so he could put it back together). Then, when it was all taken apart, he PLUGGED IT IN and began putting it back together. Twice, he ran into the house, pausing to ask me, 'Is everything okay in here?' The third time he asked, I demanded to know what was going on, so he told me that occasionally a spark (kind of like a lightning bolt) would fly from the microwave. I noticed all of our electricity was out. He fried the wiring right to the breaker box."

Wait, there's more—this one from a woman named Christine: "One of my daughters wanted to see the chicks inside eggs, so she took a carton of eggs and broke them all open, inside her closet, on top of one of my purses. No chicks. So she left the gunk there, shells and all, until I smelled it. Way too far gone to repair the purse and the carpet. Another daughter was sitting on our couch, at about four years old, and was apparently hungry (I was nursing the baby), and she climbed up on the counter and got the peanut butter. She ate with her hands watching Big Bird until she'd had enough. Then she decided to cover the couch with it like a cake with frosting and had gotten one cushion and the back and an arm covered before I got there."

And here's Rhonda: "My sixteen-year-old left a sweaty glass on the wooden coffee table, which left a ring. He read somewhere that applying heat via an iron would remove the ring. We now have a black burn stain, in the shape of an iron, in the middle of our coffee table."

Kathleen: "My seven-year-old daughter cut her eyelashes all the way down. When I asked her what happened to her beautiful long eyelashes, she said she didn't know, she just woke up like that."

Jane: "How about cotton balls that had been used with nail polish remover left on my coffee table? You can imagine how that ate through the varnish. And the ironic part is, they had a magazine out to protect from spills, but still managed to put the used cotton balls directly on my table!"

Janie: "I tore a calf muscle two weeks ago, and the doctor said I needed to wear a special soft-cast boot. I told the doctor not to worry, because I still have two left from when I broke my foot last year. I went home to find it in the garage and not one but both boots had been completely disassembled. The project? A Lego gun that shoots electricity. They needed the insulation from the outside of the boot."

And finally, Bret: "My kids ruined my sanity. Does that count?"

Yes, Bret, it does count. And welcome to my group.

# I, SUPERHERO

ONE THING I never realized before I became a parent is that I would soon develop an expansive range of amazing superpowers. This is something that most parents never tell anyone, to protect their secret identities.

So please don't tell anyone, because then I'll have to kill you.

You develop these superpowers after you've had a few "Oh sh*%" moments, after which you wonder if perhaps you can even keep your children alive to age eighteen. Here are some of my superpowers, but remember: Don't tell anyone.

### Super Vision
This is one of the most common of the Parental Superpowers. Have you ever seen a movie where the superhero keeps glancing at someone you know is the bad guy, because his funny mannerisms are revealing something to the superhero, like, he's about to pull an automatic weapon out of his pocket and start shooting up the store?

Well, that's how parents behave in a restaurant when someone places a glass near the table edge. Even though the glass is on the other side of the table, and even though it's your thirty-five-year-old friend's beverage and the kids aren't even present, you just can't stand it. You have such a strong premonition of disaster.

You keep glancing at the glass as if magically, it's going to move itself farther from the edge. It's distracting you so much you can't even stand to listen to your friend babble about her upcoming wedding reception.

Finally, you reach over, grab the glass, and move it to the center of the table. A deep feeling of peace descends on you, while your childless friend looks at you like, "What the hell are you doing?"

"Sorry," you explain. "I have children. After a few grape-juice-all-over-the grandparents'-white-carpet experiences, I've become vigilant about these things."

## Super Detection

Kids do not understand that parents have this power, which is why they tell stupid lies.

"No, I didn't eat the brownies you made for the class picnic," he says while twitching uncontrollably and kicking his foot against the table.

Of course, it didn't impede the investigation that he still has a few brownie crumbs on his upper lip and the brownie pan was found in his room, but even without this forensic evidence, you still would have known.

My son, actually, should never embark on a life of crime, because he's constantly leaving the evidence in plain view. But I don't tell him this, so I can continue to freak him out. He thinks I must have the uncanny sleuthing abilities of Sherlock Holmes, when I come and say, "I told you not to eat ramen soup, because we're going out to dinner."

And he wonders how I know, considering the soup itself is already being digested.

But, of course, all I need to do is see that the cupboard where the soup is kept has the door hanging open, the soup wrapper is left on the kitchen counter, the unwashed pot is on the stove, and the bowl and spoon are on the floor by the television.

Amazing. Doctor Watson would be proud.

## Super Hearing

Before I adopted my kids, I never thought my ears would become so tuned to whispers that I could actually hear them from another room.

Like most moms, I block out child-related noise. My kids could be running rototillers in the back yard and I wouldn't even hear them. But the moment I hear the faint sound of whispers anywhere in the house, my super hearing becomes instantly activated.

Snatches of whispered phrases like, ". . . and then let's see what happens when we do it . . ." emanating from the bathroom get my attention, because I know the results will never bring me joy—though they might to the plumber.

True story: I was standing at my kitchen sink, washing dishes, when despite the noise of the running water, I vaguely, off in the distance, heard this from the backyard: "Watch me jump off of this." I was in the midst of a daydream about a beach in Mexico, so it took me a few moments to come back to reality and process what I'd just heard.

And it rapidly occurred to me that there was nothing to jump off in the back yard except the roof.

I went flying out the door—using my super speed—in time to stop Cheetah Boy and his friend from jumping off our quite high roofline. They had climbed onto a shed and then used that to leverage themselves onto the roof.

Quite a lot of shrieking occurred, mostly by yours truly, which was followed by a trip to the doctor. I wanted the pediatrician to explain to Cheetah Boy exactly what would happen if he tried to use his as-yet-undeveloped superpowers to jump off the roof.

"You wanted to be like Superman and jump off the roof?" the doctor intoned in his manly way to my son, who nodded his head sheepishly.

"Well, I've seen many boys in the emergency room who've tried to do that," the doctor continued. "And they hit their heads and you know what happens to them?"

"What?" Cheetah Boy asked breathlessly.

The doctor leaned forward to emphasize his point. "They have to poop in their pants every day for the rest of their lives." He leaned back.

"Oooh," my son exhaled, looking horrified.

And after that, he wisely left all the superpowers to his mom.

## SCARY VOICES COME ACROSS THE PHONE LINES

WHEN you're a parent, there are certain phone calls that can never bring you good news.

One of those is, "Hi, this is the vice principal, Ms. You-Don't-Want-To-Hear-This." When the school vice principal calls, trust me, she's never, ever calling to tell you that your child just won the national spelling bee. No, the *principal* gets to make those kinds of calls.

The vice principal is the one who calls to tell you that your kid is a juvenile delinquent. She is the enforcer. She won't invite you to join the PTA. She won't ask you to speak at Careers Day. The only reason she will ever call is because your kid is in trouble.

I remember the call telling me that Cheetah Boy had

blown up the school bathroom and I "would be expected to pay for the damage."

My heart temporarily stopped beating as I thought of the army of contractors involved in that type of job.

Well, it turned out that Cheetah Boy—then a third grader—and his friend thought it would be an interesting science experiment to turn the electric hand dryers in the bathroom upside down, stuff them full of wet paper towels and soap, and turn them on to see what would happen.

"Kaboom" is what happened, but nothing was actually destroyed, even though the phone call I got was just a tiny bit testy. Cheetah Boy was assigned to do "community service" at school. I remember thinking, "Gee, I thought my kid would be older than ten before he started having to do community service."

(After Cheetah Boy cleaned up the mess, he actually enjoyed his detention: helping the school janitor for two weeks.

Another call that is sure to be no good begins, "Do you have a dog named Buddy?"

This phrase uttered into my ear means that our evil pooch has escaped the yard for the 6,509th time and is being sheltered by some kind stranger. The last time I got this call was during a blizzard in Utah, trying to navigate my brother's four-wheel-drive down Sundance Canyon without running off the invisible road. Not the time you want to hear the dog got out and the dog sitter didn't know it yet.

Another classic: "Your child's library book is overdue."

Now, I don't know about your house, but mine is just the tiniest bit cluttered. Okay, who am I kidding—entire families could be living in it and we might not notice. We also have a lot of books. So the news that a library book hasn't been turned in is problematic because it prompts the question: Well, then where is it?

Usually, after five or six hours of searching, the book is

located, but only after I ground the kids to their rooms and refuse to let them do anything else until it happens. Usually, the offender is Cheetah Boy, though it can be irksome to discover that Curly Girl has checked out six books on cocker spaniels and they're all overdue.

And then there's this one that begins, "Now, your son is all right, but this is the school nurse and . . ."

Cheetah Boy is such an active kid that he's smashing some part of his body on an almost daily basis. I should start buying a Christmas present for the school nurse, I think, because I talk to her more often than some members of my family.

The worst was when he fell off an exercise bike—can you believe they have exercise bikes for sixth graders?—at school, and it looked like he had broken his femur. Fortunately for my sanity, the school couldn't get hold of me for about a half-hour, and during that time, they found he only had a scrape. But he got the fun of being removed from the building in a wheelchair while everyone gathered around.

All of this makes me wonder: Why can't anyone ever call me to say, "You've come into an inheritance from a long-lost relative"?

## IN PRAISE OF PARENTAL MELTDOWNS

THERE ARE times when children just drive their parents bonkers. As one of my friends used to say, "Raising kids is like being nibbled to death by ducks."

Every parent sometimes simply goes insane and does things that are completely socially unacceptable. No, I don't mean you can wallop your kids and feel okay about it. I do mean the occasional freakout is not abnormal. It happens to good, caring parents—not just to the ones who end up on

Jerry Springer.

One night, I got in such a battle with my Type A adolescent son over who runs our house that I started throwing his things out into the back patio. One at a time, I threw things while loudly demanding that he acknowledge I was the boss. (I hasten to add that I didn't throw anything he treasures, like his sports trophies.)

His possessions made a loud crash as each one hit the concrete, while I demanded, "Who's the boss?" Only after he finally agreed, "You're the boss, you're the boss," did I stop. And then I made him clean up the mess.

I felt bad about this for some time afterward, because I didn't need a psychology degree to know that a better parent would have handled it differently. But I know I'm not alone. Others have also lost their marbles in the parenting game—and I have proof, in the form of confessions that readers of my column have shared with me. Here are a few—and while not many of us can say we approve, I bet we certainly can relate:

"I threw out my son's Halloween candy and said there had been an ant invasion."

"A few months ago, my son had a little plastic dart gun. After I told him not to point it, he promptly shot his little brother, very narrowly missing his eye. I calmly took the gun, put it in a big Ziploc bag, took out the meat whacker, and smashed it to pieces. My son thinks I overreacted. I don't think so."

"Once I was totally exasperated with how my son was behaving while I was making breakfast for three kids on my own. So I poured a pitcher of orange juice over his head. It wasn't well thought-out, but it did keep me from doing anything more regrettable, and it did change the tone of the morning into a calm, 'Oh, my, we did push Dad over the edge, didn't we?'"

"When I was a police patrol sergeant, I got a call from some officers who had found a dad and his two kids sleeping on the pavement in an industrial area. Apparently, there was a discussion at home that got very heated about taking your studies seriously or you would end up living in the streets. When the kid said something smart, both kids got packed up to spend the night on the sidewalk. I understood the teaching moment, and told the officer to leave them there. The other homeless in the area said they would make sure they were all right."

"My husband threw my son's laptop and broke it. They got into an argument right after my son had been kicked out of school for smoking pot on campus. They were nose-to-nose and when my husband grabbed my son's laptop and slammed it onto the floor in the hallway."

Personally, I remember every single time I've ever lost my mind and acted like a big jerk for one simple reason: The kids remind me.

"Mommy," they begin, "remember the time you . . ." And then they laugh and laugh.

I'm glad we can all laugh about it today. Because it didn't seem funny at the time.

## PARENTS, STAND UP FOR YOUR RIGHTS

I HAVE decided to form a new group to protect the legal rights of oppressed parents everywhere, because it's too easy to forget you actually do have rights when you're in a heated dispute with your kids.

As the founding member of Parents Are Not Too Stupid (PANTS), I am providing this handy reference guide, similar to the ACLU wallet card describing a citizen's civil rights.

For beleaguered parents everywhere, I suggest you laminate this and carry it with you at all times. Be strong. Stand up for your rights.

You have the right to . . .

- Remain silent the fifth time your child asks you why he can't do something.
- Make unreasonable searches and seizures of your child's backpack.
- Ask to see the evidence, especially involving promises that you allegedly made but don't remember.
- Private time in the bathroom without having to listen to "Mommy mommy mommy mommy mommy mommy mommy mommy mommy mommy" from right outside the door.
- Refuse to accept hearsay about what siblings supposedly did or did not do.
- Declare "Bedtime" just because they are getting on your nerves.
- Confiscate cell phones without a warrant or prior warning.
- Refuse to consent to any activities that occur before 8 a.m. on a Saturday.
- Make sandwiches for dinner when you're not feeling well.
- Make one telephone call, uninterrupted by children demanding to know when you're going to be off the phone.
- Stop the car and make everyone sit on the curb until they agree to shut up and stop aggravating you. (I once did this on the way to the San Diego Zoo.)
- Answer "Because I told you so" without any justification whatsoever.

# MORE PANTS

HELLO, parents. How are you today? Welcome to our meeting of Parents Are Not Too Stupid (PANTS). Pull up a chair and have a seat. There are some cookies and punch on the table, so help yourselves. We all appreciate the time you are taking out of your busy day to come. Hopefully the traffic wasn't too bad.

If this is your first time here, please raise your hand.

We always start our meetings by taking a deep, cleansing breath.

Breathe in. Breathe out.

Feel the stress leaving your body.

All those fights over homework. Gone. Arguments over the cell phone. Gone. Aggravation over who took the missing scissors. Gone.

That's right. Just bless them and release them. Feel them flying away from you on wings of gold.

Now, it's time for our affirmations. All parents need these every day.

So please stand and repeat after me in unison:

• Other people value my opinion.
• My jokes are funny.
• My clothes are modest yet never out of style.
• I am a great dancer.
• My singing is wonderful.
• My jeans fit exactly right.
• I am an intelligent person whom others ask for advice.
• My cooking is delicious.
• I am not a control freak.
• My new hairstyle looks wonderful.
• I am fun to be with and others enjoy my company.
• Our house looks perfectly normal.
• It's okay to put Baileys in my coffee at any time of the

day or night.

Thanks, parents. How do you feel? Better?

If you have teenagers, we recommend doing these twice a day. Now, we have time left over if you want to add a few affirmations of your own. And we'll post these online, too, so you can print them out. If you tape them on your mirror, you can repeat them to yourselves every day.

Or a few times a day, if you have teenagers.

And check on the bulletin board on the way out for information about our hotline. Trained volunteers are available twenty-four hours a day to repeat these affirmations with you. And, hey, parents. You are wonderful. You are special. You are doing a great job.

## THE EDUCATION WE NEED

ONE MORNING, my son had to memorize the "five themes of geography" for a class. Let's face it: There is no situation in adult life where anyone will ever have to know that geography has more than four themes. Like algebra, which I couldn't do now even if it were the only thing that would save me from burning hellfire, some things that you learn in school are just useless. And you never get to study topics you actually need.

Here are some real-life classes we could all use. If you think you're qualified to teach any of them, send me your résumé and I'll see what I can do..

### Guilt 101

Regrettably, I can't pretend that I spent thirty-six hours in agonizing labor giving birth to my children, since they were already potty-trained when I adopted them. And, while I have a very short fuse, I really am no good at pouting or cold-shouldering. I need a psychology practicum on the use of guilt as an effective method of discipline and lifetime control. The successful outcome of the class would be when someone asks me how many moms it takes to screw in a light bulb, I can say with weary sincerity, "None. I'll just sit in the dark."

## Workshop: Avoiding Verbal Traps

Children spend a lot of time trying to trap you into promising things they want. In fact, they will often even insist that you did promise something, when you know perfectly well that you didn't. This practical vocabulary course will allow you to practice the use of certain useful words and phrases. You'll practice saying, "Maybe," "I'll think about it," "Ask me tomorrow," and "Hmm" until they automatically replace any tendency to say yes or okay.

## Drug-Use Detection for Dummies

How to use a home drug test. How to ransack your kid's drawers for fun and profit. How to train your dog at home to search for drugs and when to bring in the K-9 unit. How to mark the liquor in your cabinet so the kids can't just dilute it.

## Classic Mommyisms, Graduate Seminar

This course will provide the opportunity to recall and practice catchphrases from the Early Classic period of parenting, many of which you swore you would never use on your own children. Bring your own phrases and learn some new ones! We'll trade experiences and rehearse the proper inflections. Classic example: I hope someday your child does the same thing to you, then you'll know what it feels like.

## An Overview of the Perfect Mommy Syndrome

This anthropology course will deal with the perfect mommy culture and examine its causes and its failures. We will look at growing evidence that Perfect Mommies, who appear to be ideal parents on the outside, actually drink a quart of vodka a day, have recurring ulcers, and shout at their kids when no one can hear. The class will also hear from women who used to be Perfect Mommies, but abandoned that life-style to live blissfully in sloth.

### Ph.D. Dissertation: Letting Go

How to allow your child to grow up and away from you gracefully. How to wear a frozen smile and bite your lip while watching your child make the same stupid mistakes that you made, and for which you paid dearly. This class will include the opportunity to learn new hobbies and crafts to fill your empty hours, and to keep your hands occupied while your child is out late with the car. Again.

## WANT KIDS TO DO CHORES? GO BACK TO BED

I DISCOVERED this method of getting my kids to do their chores completely by accident. One day, it was almost time to take Cheetah Boy to baseball practice, and I told him to unload the dishwasher before we left. Well, he didn't want to unload the dishwasher, so he sat down on the kitchen floor and started having a fit about child labor and the general unfairness of it all.

Normally I would have talked to him, argued with him, reasoned with him. But I was really tired that day. So I just told him, "You don't want to do your chores and I don't blame you. I don't want to do my chores either. One of my chores is taking you to baseball practice. And since no one feels like doing chores today, let's don't. I'll go back to bed instead."

And I did. I crawled into bed, and, might I add, it felt very good, too.

Well, Cheetah Boy was in my room quickly, sitting on my bed, begging me to get up and take him to practice. In fact, he was begging me to let him do the chore that he had refused to do only minutes before.

I told him he could unload the dishwasher while I thought it over. And stayed in bed until he was done.

That's how I discovered that going back to bed is a great technique for getting my kids to do their chores if they're balking. It only works if there's somewhere they want to go that you were going to take them.

Now, fortunately, I usually don't even have to get into bed, I just have to sigh, turn away, and start heading for the bedroom, and they're begging me to stop and change my mind. No yelling, no fighting, just passive resistance. Sort of like how Gandhi freed India. Give it a try. It works.

## WHY DIDN'T ANYONE TELL ME?

BEING a mom has been a beautiful experience, mostly, when I don't feel like I'm headed for a padded room.

There are things, though, I wish people had warned me about. As you know by now, I got into the game late and didn't get an owner's manual. It just would have been nice if someone had told me that:

1. Your child will never willingly put on outerwear of any kind, not a coat or hat, or use an umbrella before age thirty-five, at least not in Southern California. Just take a deep, cleansing breath and let it go. And, yes, they will wear flip-flops in the rain. When my kids complain about being cold, I just look at them and say, "I have no pity for self-inflicted wounds."

2. Kids will not voluntarily starve to death. I knew a mom who fretted herself into a frenzy because her finicky son

was going to camp, and she was sure he would pass out from malnourishment. Well, guess what? He ate heartily until he came home, then he turned on the finicky act again. My kids turned up their noses at Thai food until we went to Thailand and there was nothing else to eat. Guess what? They discovered they loved it.

3. They need to participate in sports. If your precious ones don't like team sports, get them into tennis or running or swimming. Don't make it optional. Their bodies need exercise. I tried to convince my daughter's best friends to join her basketball, soccer, and softball teams, and their moms would always just roll their eyes and say, "Oh, she doesn't like that." Really? She never tried it. How do you know she wouldn't love it? However, don't encourage horseback riding unless you're as rich as Bill Gates. My friend's daughter rides English, and it's bankrupting her.

4. You will never again own white furniture. I walked past a lovely white couch in the window of a furniture store in Laguna Beach the other day and pondered the mystery of who would buy it. People who have houses so big they can ban kids and dogs from entering certain rooms or people who don't have either. But then, it's not always the kids—I spilled red wine on the only white couch I ever owned ten minutes after I took the plastic off.

5. Your kids don't have to like you. If they don't hate your guts occasionally, you're not doing it right. Yeah, yeah, you need to be sensitive to their tender little feelings and all that, but sometimes they just need to suck it up, and you need to make them. I'm always amazed when I hear parents say, "Well, Junior doesn't want to do that." Who on God's green earth cares what five-year-old Junior wants? Get in the car, kid. You're going. And if I find out you're one of those parents who lets teenage kids have parties with liquor, I will personally come over and kick

your pants off. What are you teaching them? To break the law?

6. Any of your kids locked in the closet right now? Any of them have rickets? Do you beat them with a strap? Do you berate them and call them names? Are you drunk when they come home? Do you leave them with the nanny and stay out until ten o'clock at night? If not, then you're probably not a bad parent. Failing to make your child's preschool graduation does not make you a bad parent. But failing to make their high school graduation probably does.

7. They grow up ridiculously fast. It's all over in the blink of an eye, my friends. Don't think you'll spend time with your kid later, because there isn't any later. There is only now. Someday, when you're on your deathbed, you won't regret the times you missed work, but you will regret the times you didn't spend with your children. Even if it means sitting through the longest, most boring Little League game of all time. In Simi Valley. When it's 111 degrees. And the coach is yelling at you because you keep running out and putting cold towels on your son's neck. Oh, sorry. Sudden flashback.

8. Ignore the peanut gallery. People who don't have kids always seem to know the best ways to raise children, and they're happy to share that with you, any time of day or night. Ditto with old folks who've forgotten what their own kids were like. Don't be embarrassed. When your baby cries on the plane, just remind yourself of the 1,112 times you had to sit and listen to other people's crying babies. Now it's your turn. I remember being in a restaurant in Yucca Valley when my kids were little. I was blissfully happy that, for once, they were sitting nicely in their chairs and weren't running around wreaking havoc on the establishment. Then I saw some crabby older woman

glaring at them like they'd killed her dog. I looked over at my son, and he was very quietly shredding napkins into a neat little pile. Get over yourself, lady. I was just happy my kid had a new hobby.

9. They need to do chores. Yes, I know it's easier to do the housework yourself than to make them do it. But unless they have a trust fund, your children will actually need to know how to clean things. When we went to Costa Rica, my kids were the only ones who could cook. How are these young adults going to survive, my friends, if they don't know how to do common household tasks?

And, always remember:

10. Never let them see you sweat.

Yes, it's scary. But you can do it, my friends. You can do it.

# 3

# BUDDY
# THE WONDER DOG

## I GOT DUPED INTO
## TAKING HOME A SCRUFFY PUP

I ACQUIRED Buddy the Wonder Dog, a scruffy little terrier from the pound, after eons of painful and protracted begging from my daughter. Curly Girl threatened to hold her breath until she turned blue or she got a dog, whichever came first, and eventually the American Lung Society made me give in.

Okay, I made that part up; she didn't actually hold her breath. But my friend Teri really did threaten to report me for child cruelty if I didn't get that girl a dog, even though I personally think dogs are only good with sauerkraut and mustard.

But Curly Girl is also horse crazy, and I figured I would save money, because a dog is at least marginally cheaper than a horse, plus easier to clean up after. There's no pretense that the dog we eventually obtained will ever pull a carriage or do anything else useful, except maybe annoy the neighbors I don't like.

At first, I thought I'd get a pooch from one of those groups that do good work by rescuing dogs from death, bailing them out of the shelter. I figured by getting a dog from one of these dedicated animal-lovers, at least I'd know something about the beast before I brought it home to chew up my furniture and maim my two small children.

I filled out countless dog adoption forms and sent eleven thousand emails, but every single rescue place rejected me, apparently because I admitted I wanted the dog for my daughter and didn't pretend I wanted it to sleep on a velvet pillow next to me and dine at the table on solid gold plates.

At least I never got a rejection like my friend Liz, who got turned down by a golden retriever rescue group because--and I'm not making this up--she doesn't have a pool.

In fact, it was harder to adopt a dog from one of those

rescue groups than it was for me to adopt my two kids, because I did eventually adopt Cheetah Boy and Curly Girl
through the state. I never succeeded in getting a rescue dog,
although I did get so far as to have an interview with one dog
in a park.

Even though I was on time, wore a suit, and had a clean
copy of my résumé, apparently, Benji didn't like my looks, or
maybe I was wearing the wrong shoes, because his doggie
foster mom decided against me.

I did all this secretly, by the way, because I didn't want
to get the kids excited before I knew whether I would come
to my senses and bail out of the search.

Finally, I gave up on the dog rescue groups and just
went to my local animal shelter by myself. I was looking for
a smallish pooch who was house-trained and would be good
with kids.

I was emotionally prepared for the animal shelter after
going to many state-run "adoption fairs," where they put foster kids on display sort of like at the pound, hoping adoptive
parents will be drawn to pick them.

Eventually, I picked out a cute, scruffy, orange-and-
white terrier, who was so hyped-up at being released from
the cage he couldn't sit still to be petted. Instead, he jumped
four feet into the air every 10 seconds, like he was on a pogo
stick or maybe trying to catch a passing helicopter.

Inside, when I asked the shelter workers to hold him for
me until I could come back with the kids, they looked at me
quizzically. "You realize this is a very high-energy dog," they
said to me, looking stern.

"That's okay," I said. "I have very high-energy kids."
After discussing the fact that this particular pooch was an
escape artist, could scale chain-link fences and had already
been back to the pound once as a runaway, I still liked him
for some unaccountable reason.

I drove over to pick up my kids at two-thirty in the afternoon and told them we were going somewhere special as a surprise.

They got it into their heads that this meant ice cream, and thus were devastated when we passed the ice cream parlor and kept going. I ignored the rapid-fire, Gestapo-like questioning from the back seat, which got more and more intense as we went along.

Finally, as we drove into the shelter parking lot, Curly Girl saw the sign that said "Animal Adoptions."

She started sobbing and said, "Mommy! You're getting me a dog!"

I started tearing up and then looked over to see her brother, Cheetah Boy, also crying, but for a different reason.

"We can't get a dog," Cheetah Boy said. "He'll be mean to our cat!"

Our tuxedo cat, Jeeves, was sweet but timid, and Cheetah Boy was especially attached to him. I promised we'd get a dog that liked cats, but Cheetah Boy could not stop crying as we went into the pound. So I had one kid crying on either side of me, for opposite reasons.

The shelter workers put the dog, which they called Beetle Bailey, into a pen, and we went in with him. Beetle Bailey again began jumping as if he were on a trampoline, dashing any hopes I had that petting him might soothe my son.

Curly Girl was cautiously optimistic, though, and the shelter worker said we could do a "cat test" on Beetle Bailey, to know how he reacted to feline friends.

We watched through a window as she put the dog into a room with a cat. Beetle Bailey promptly ran under a bench and pooped.

"Well, that's good, because he's afraid of cats," I told the kids. "He'll stay away from Jeeves."

Somewhat mollified, Cheetah Boy stopped sobbing but

still refused to be optimistic.

I filled out the paperwork, agreed to make a lifetime commitment to a strange animal, plunked down a hundred bucks, and then we went home, after buying a leash and some food.

On the way home, we decided we should call him Buddy instead of Beetle Bailey, especially since no one under the age of seventy has any idea who Beetle Bailey was.

When we got home, Buddy seemed excited to see his new house. One of his first activities was to find Jeeves and bark ferociously at him. And bark. And bark. And bark. He was as persistent as a televangelist to whom you mistakenly gave your phone number.

Eventually, we discovered that Buddy is a long-haired Jack Russell terrier, and that he wasn't going to hurt Jeeves, but he was going to bark at him ceaselessly.

Forever.

It wasn't long before Jeeves decided to hit the highway, moving into our neighbor's yard, despite the fact that our neighbor didn't actually want him to live with her.

And I realized we'd been bamboozled by a dog who tricked us into bringing him home under false pretenses, after which it was too late to take him back. After all, we'd already named him. And bought the leash and dog bowl. And, today, even though I gaze longingly at other people's cats, I guess we are now a dog household for a long time to come.

## LIFE WITH AN INDY DOG ISN'T EASY

IF YOU happen to see a little orange-and-white blur pass you on the sidewalk at approximately the speed of light, it's probably Buddy. We should have named this creature Houdini when we brought him home from the pound, because he has figured out every way possible to escape from our home and yard into the wide world beyond.

Watching us chase our dog has become one of the neighborhood hobbies, so the yells of "Buddy's loose" bring all the neighbors out onto their lawns, to place bets on who will win, place, and show.

This is ironic because I never even wanted a canine pal to begin with. I don't actually hate dogs, you understand. I have even been known occasionally to pet one, if absolutely necessary.

Buddy is absurdly cute and quite sweet, in most other ways a great dog, which is why no one suspects that he has a Dark Side. I can't even tell you what we've done to persuade this animal to stay safely at home. I have memorized every episode of "Dog Whisperer." Now I tell Buddy that I "own the space" around the front door and when I walk in or out, he better stay back. Sometimes it even works.

We had to reinforce our fence because he pushed the metal gate posts apart, so he could squeeze between them.

He actually even figured out how to use an old discarded rubber swimming pool, piled up on the side of our house, as a trampoline to vault himself over the block wall into the neighbor's yard, where he could escape. These are neighbors who dislike us, so it was particularly vexing that we couldn't figure out how he kept getting into their yard, until we spied on him and caught him doing it.

We took him to obedience training, where he proved to have doggie ADHD and got exiled to the back row reserved for naughty dogs that wouldn't pay attention.

We take him on walks, so he has plenty of officially approved opportunities to enjoy the neighborhood. Occasionally, he goes to the dog park.

None of that matters, because the darn dog just likes to run, run, run.

And, when he is hauling it, that animal is fast. It's kind of like watching the Indy 500. You can see flames licking up from his heels as he pounds the pavement, always well ahead of his hollering chasers. If he didn't stop occasionally to relieve himself, or pause to say hi to another dog, he would have made it to Canada by now or been squashed by a car trying.

The other day, Curly Girl took Buddy for a walk before she left for school. Her brother and I were still in pajamas. As Curly Girl left for school, a great shout arose, and it became immediately obvious that Indy Car Buddy was off yet again. Curly Girl began chasing him down the street on foot while sounding the alarm. Still in his pajama bottoms, bare chested, my son Cheetah Boy then ran outside, jumped on his bike and began chasing him, too.

Our neighbor Tim, who was at that moment pulling out of his driveway to go to work, saw what was happening and also joined the chase in his car.

I was still in the house, in my bathrobe, when I heard all the commotion and, in an action that has become sadly familiar, I grabbed my keys and leaped into my 4Runner, barefoot, and also began chasing the pooch at the end of this procession.

So we had this ridiculous lineup like the Keystone Kops, all of us chasing one terror of a terrier who thought it was the most fun he'd had in years. When we finally caught up with him—which only happened when he finally stopped to whiz on a bush—he had the most self-satisfied grin on his face, as if he knew the entire neighborhood had been in pursuit and he had beaten them all. I think he was saying to himself, "Well, even race cars have to make a pit stop occasionally."

While this is a very aggravating problem and our big fear is that Buddy will get hit by a car, I do understand how he feels. I pretty much have the wanderlust bug myself.

If this dog were at Alcatraz, he would have jumped in the bay and tried to swim a long time ago.

He's just a dog with a lust for adventure. Which makes him fit into our family just right. If I could only teach him to cross at the light, maybe I wouldn't even mind so much.

## BUDDY THE FREELOADER

THERE'S one member of our household who does not pull his weight around here, even though that's only twenty-four pounds.

Buddy hasn't done a single chore since we got him. Well, I take that back. He is very good at cleaning up the kitchen floor if I drop a piece of chicken on it. But other than that, not a one.

I've had earnest discussions with him over this point. I've even demonstrated to him some of the ways he could help out around here. For example, he could increase security by barking at strangers who come into the yard. He completely ignores any human being who comes near our house, except to try to lick them to death if they come inside the door. I shouldn't really tell you this, in case you're a burglar, but the only things that our so-called "watchdog" actually watches are dogs, cats, and other furry creatures.

This came to mind a few days ago, when he barked for nine hours and twenty-seven minutes at an opossum the size of a Range Rover in our backyard. He then got into a hissing, yelping spat with the creature, requiring me to get out of bed and hose them off to break them up.

I couldn't help noting that, earlier that day, our yard had been full of strangers, none of whom he barked at even for a millisecond.

As I sat in the vet's office, making sure the opossum

hadn't bitten him (answer: no, but it still cost me $70 because everything always does), it reminded me that I really do need to find a way to get that dog to pay for himself.

Buddy looks identical to that performing pooch from the movie *The Artist*. And also similar to Eddie, the dog from *Frasier*. Even if I don't want to send him to canine acting school, he could get a job in Vegas as a celebrity impersonator.

If he can root around in the trash and find every meat scrap dumped there, why can't he find some of the socks, scissors, forks, and spoons that are always missing around this house?

I'd be willing to pay him a finder's fee.

I've been racking my brain trying to think of a way to monetize his superior jumping skills, but other than selling him to the circus, nothing immediately comes to mind.

Jack Russell terriers were bred in England as fox-hunting dogs by a guy named . . . wait for it . . . Jack Russell. Their job was to find the fox and corner it in its den, without harming it, and just bark at it unceasingly until the hunter rode up and took over. Since we have a well-publicized shortage of foxes in our neighborhood, this isn't terribly useful to me.

Buddy's other skills include annoying people at the dog park by humping their large dogs, due to what appears to be a canine Napoleon complex; devising eighty-seven ways to get past our fence; and running fast.

The only one of those that's been useful is the running. My kids will actually put a halter on him and let him pull them on their scooters and skateboards. More than one driver has nearly crashed watching Buddy the Wonder Dog pulling a kid down the street.

We like this because it's the only thing that gets this dog tired. Maybe I can build some kind of dogcart and sell rides. That way, he's not only pulling his weight, but someone else's. Then I can use the money to pay the vet for the next time he finds that opossum.

# THE DOG LEFT THE LIGHTS ON AGAIN

IT'S MYSTIFYING to me how Buddy could constantly be leaving lights on all over the house, as well as electronic devices that no one is using. See, I just opened my power bill and felt a little electric shock go up and down my body when I saw the "Amount Now Due," which was more than tuition for my entire first semester at college.

I keep trying to make my children understand that a light switch that can be flipped up to turn it on can (and this is the amazing part) also be flipped down, to turn it off.

This concept seems to completely evade them.

Both of my teenagers have jimmied their cellphones to connect with aliens living on Saturn. They can figure out how to get direct video from the White House situation room. But they haven't really learned how to operate the "OFF" switch on their many electronic devices, when they're not watching, playing, tapping, or listening to them. Nor on the lamps or light fixtures in our home.

They don't admit this, of course. Instead, they blame everything on the dog.

Buddy obviously is a big power waster. It's already bad enough that I have to personally pay $3 billion toward the cost of shutting down the San Onofre nuclear power plant. Well, okay, I don't really have to pay the entire $3 billion, which is good because my checking account only has $1.33 in it. (But that's what we customers collectively are getting stuck with, after massive screwups by Southern California Edison and its contractors that led to the plant being shut down.)

And, then, there are my kids' weird nighttime habits. For

years now, my son has insisted on sleeping with the overhead fan in his bedroom going full blast, regardless of the
season.

Now that it's chilly at night, he still revs it up, turning
his room into something of an icebox by morning. He's buried under the covers, I might add, but the electric meter is
just humming happily along. Why does he do this? It seems
very odd to me. I can't get him to stop, either.

Now his sister has also started leaving her overhead fan
on all night. The temperatures are getting down to fifty degrees in the winter around here. It's not exactly Buffalo, but
it's certainly cold enough to dispense with the services of
a fan. I suppose I could respond by just removing the fans,
and it may come to that. But what would Buddy do?

## ONE BUDDY IS ENOUGH

A FEW days ago, Curly Girl and I were lying on the couch,
stimulating our brains by watching reruns of "America's
Next Top Model," when the doorbell rang. Curly Girl ran to
answer it, as kids always do, but I didn't pay any attention,
because I figured it was one of their neighborhood friends.
(Childhood is the last time in your life you will actually want
to answer the door or the phone, unless it's Ed McMahon
with the Publisher's Clearing House Giveaway—and he's
dead now, right?)

Curly Girl closed the door behind her and announced
excitedly, "I have a little doggy who got out!" She promptly
brought over a shaggy little Jack Russell terrier.

Since Buddy regularly makes prison breaks from our
yard, this wasn't surprising in the least, except that when
Curly Girl walked over with a dog in her arms, it was smaller
and had a mysterious big black spot on its rear end.

"Hey, that's not Buddy," I said, winning the Albert

Einstein award.

Indeed, for once it was not the evil one, but an impostor. After I finished exclaiming over this, it occurred to me to say, "Hey! Give that dog back right now!" But too late, the neighbor who had brought the pooch over in the understandable belief that it was ours had decamped rapidly, leaving us with one extra dog, sans collar.

Since it was Sunday afternoon, I told Curly Girl to put a harness on the spare dog and we'd take him over to the animal shelter, since his owner would certainly be looking for him. Those dogs can run a long way so there was no way of knowing where he came from. Curly Girl gave me one imploring look that said, "Can't we keep him?" but I just glowered and got the car keys.

I snapped a picture of him first, so we could put up "Found Dog" fliers, and then we got in the car and started heading to the animal shelter.

Within two blocks, we drove past a woman in a huge SUV who was driving slowly, looking dazed and confused. Since I know that condition well, I rolled down my window and said, "Are you by chance looking for a dog?"

When she said she was, I said, "Well, we happen to have an extra dog." She looked overjoyed to see the mutt and said that he'd just gotten out without his collar.

"He's only seven months old and we've tried everything to train him, but he keeps running away," she said. I told her to get used to it and get some good pet insurance, though I should have asked her why on Earth he wasn't wearing a collar. We exchanged addresses in case someday we again find ourselves with an extra Jack Russell terrier on our hands.

And I drove away, thanking the almighty that the dog was safe and, more importantly, our household wasn't stuck with a second dog. Believe me, one Buddy is enough.

# LIL WAYNE MOVES IN

SO MY teenage daughter has been yelling at me a lot lately, and it's all because of our new pooch. We got this fluffy white dog from the pound in June because my daughter insisted she just had to have another beast, in addition to Buddy the Wonder Dog.

Some people have told me he's a Bichon Frise, and I like this idea because those dogs cost over a thousand bucks from a breeder, and it means we got a bargain. I think he looks like a Maltipoo. However, others have suggested he's just a GWD, a "generic white dog," and that may be true, too.

My kids have been pestering me to get another dog, even though Buddy, at age fourteen, is still quite spry.

Cheetah Boy was in favor of a new dog, but he wanted a huge dog that would look badass and scare potential robbers. For this reason, he wasn't allowed to go to the pound with me to look for our new addition, because he kept picking out mastiffs and pit bulls and then grumbling when I said no. Big dogs eat a lot and then excrete a lot, and I didn't want to deal with it on either end.

I picked out an adorable little black-and-white terrier who looked like she could star in her own movie. She may have been the cutest dog who ever lived. But the people at the animal shelter require you to bring in your current dogs to see if they get along with the new pet, and for some reason, this animal just hated Buddy on sight.

She wouldn't stop growling at him, like he was Donald Trump and she was Rosie O'Donnell.

So that deal fell through. But then Curly Girl found this walking ball of fur who'd clearly been living on the streets for months, because he was overgrown and matted. You could barely tell there was an actual dog under all that filthy fluff.

He was shaking so hard and terrified of everything that

it took the shelter workers 10 minutes just to get a leash on him. But when he finally got out onto the lawn with Buddy, they didn't hate each other.

We decided to bring him home.

I arranged to have him bathed and clipped before he was neutered, paid $153 in fees, and we drove over to fetch him at the vet's the following Monday, after his puppy-siring years had been abruptly cut short.

We were fully expecting the new dog to be cowering in terror, as he had been in the shelter, especially after being groomed, shaven, and snipped in his personal, private places. But from the moment we picked him up, he was obviously so happy to be in someone's lap and going home, he couldn't stop licking Curly Girl. He made it clear that he owned her, and also every square inch of his new house.

To placate my son, who wasn't happy that our new dog weighed only fourteen pounds, we named him Lil Wayne after one of his favorite rappers. That name has the added benefit of identifying the age of anyone who stops to greet him, because older people invariably think he's named for Wayne Newton, whereas younger people laugh, because it's so incongruous to have a small, fluffy white dog named after this notorious rapper.

Buddy ignored the interloper when he first moved in, but eventually succumbed to his youthful enthusiasm. Buddy never cared much for other dogs, but now he and Lil Wayne play together like brothers, and he's so much more energetic and full of life, it's a wonder to behold.

Lil Wayne is as cute as an animated stuffed animal and wants nothing more than to sit on your lap and lick you every minute of every day. And he's a bundle of energy, so it's like raising a two-year-old, appropriate because he is actually around two.

Curly Girl started taking him to Doggie Manners classes

on Saturday mornings, which is why she's been yelling at me. When Lil Wayne jumps on me a hundred twenty-seven times a day, I tell him to "get down." Apparently, that's bad. I'm supposed to just tell him "No." Because "down" is a different command.

"Stop telling him that!" she will yell at me. "He won't know what to do!"

I think to myself, "Well, I know what to do, which is beat the tar out of you for yelling at your sainted mother, who does everything for you."

But I don't say that, and I'd never beat the tar out of her anyway, not even if I knew what that expression meant.

She's been telling me that I need to train this dog, too, and I suppose that's true, because when she moves out, I'll probably be stuck with him. Good thing he's so cute.

## HELP!
## I'VE BECOME ONE OF THOSE PEOPLE

I'M A little frightened right now, because of what happened on Christmas morning.

While we were all gathered around, watching *A Christmas Story*, eating cinnamon rolls (they have no calories on Christmas Day. Look it up. It's a fact) and opening presents, it suddenly occurred to me that I hadn't bought any gifts for the dogs.

I felt sad. And a little bit guilty. I couldn't even look at Buddy or Lil Wayne, because I was too sad that they had no gifts to open. No cute doggie stockings from the pet store. No special treats. No new toys.

And, then, suddenly, I was terrified. I realized I was becoming one of those people. You know the ones.

I knew this because only a few days earlier, I'd

contemplated going to the shockingly overpriced doggie boutique and buying them raincoats, even though God gave them raincoats they'd worn successfully for years, also known as fur.

You need to understand I'm a world-class cheapskate. If they were handing out badges for skinflints, I'd wear mine proudly, take a picture of it, and post it on my Facebook page. I had a lengthy conversation with my son this morning about the cheapest place to buy Colgate toothpaste. I drive twenty five minutes to the Arabic market to get cheaper produce. Only a year ago, I would have rolled my eyes and scoffed at the idea of buying Christmas presents for animals.

"I keep those useless beasts around and feed them, even though they don't earn their keep," I would have said. "I had to pay money to bring them home from the pound and give them a nice place to live and chew up my shoes. That's all they need."

So it felt like a watershed moment (or it would have if I even knew what that meant) when I realized I'm starting to think of these dogs as my children. Even though I still have two young adult children at home, tugging on my heart and my purse strings daily. I mean, it's one thing to let out your maternal urges on your pooch if you don't actively have children pestering you at home. That, I can understand.

Go ahead, buy Fido those ski goggles and the special doggie backpack so you can take him wherever you go, before you bring him home to his heated bed and fix him his own special chicken and rice for dinner. He'll love you for it.

And, in the interest of full disclosure, I couldn't help looking at heated dog beds for Buddy, now that he's old and arthritic. See what I mean? I don't even have a heated bed, and I'm considering buying one for a dog.

Yup, becoming one of those people. Not a dog owner, but a pet parent.

Listen, I've been in countries where people would love to eat what we give our dogs. So I never thought I'd be a person who spoiled my pooch. But somehow, here I am. Contemplating exactly what kind of raincoat to get for my small furry beasts. Should I get a Sherlock Holmes outfit, complete with deerstalker? Or maybe a little fireman's outfit? I'm not really sure how the dogs will react.

I bought Buddy some socks to wear (see? one of those people) that were supposed to help keep him from slipping on my hardwood floors. Ha ha ha ha ha ha. They stayed on his feet exactly forty-two seconds. Well, he got the front ones off in twenty seconds, and the back ones in sixty-two seconds, so I averaged it out. Thinking about getting socks for your dog? Here's a tip: Don't. Though it was almost worth it for the hilarious sight of a ticked-off dog trying to walk in socks for the first time. He did not approve.

Nowadays, I don't even buy socks for my son, because he's twenty-two years old and still loses them constantly. But I'll buy them for my dog.

I try not to ponder this too deeply.

I know some of you are thinking that—with my attitude—I don't even deserve a dog. And I agree that while my dogs don't do a darn thing around here to earn their keep, they are always happy to see me when I come home, and that counts for something. They never ask me for money (though they beg so often for food you'd think they're malnourished), they never change the radio station in the car, and they seldom leave their socks in the hallway for me to pick up.

Well, except for Buddy. He did leave his socks there, but only the once.

# 4

# SURVIVING THE TEEN YEARS

## PARENTING TEENS IS OUT OF THIS WORLD

WHEN Cheetah Boy turned fourteen and Curly Girl was twelve, I realized that I would have to learn how to be a mom all over again.

The problem with being the parent of teenagers is you have a whole new series of things to worry about. Yes, they could still get run over in the street. But now, there are entire categories of other things they could be doing in the streets that are also dangerous and over which I have little control. I've got a stack of books on my coffee table about how to parent teenagers, and even after having read them all, I still feel like it would be easier to fly the space shuttle to the moon. Wonder if I can fit into that astronaut suit and learn to live on freeze-dried food? At least I wouldn't have to listen to teenybopper music every time I get in the car. Unless they have teenagers in space.

## BRACE YOURSELF FOR THE PAIN

EVERY culture has its bizarre coming-of-age rituals. In Vanuatu, adolescent boys dive headfirst off towers, with ropes tied to their ankles to save them from certain death. Brazilian girls of the Tukuna tribe are painted with black dye and throw firebrands at symbolic demons. In the Amazon, boys of a certain tribe are initiated into manhood by sticking their hands into mittens woven of viciously biting ants.

In our country, the most common rite of passage also involves pain and sacrifice.

It's called orthodontia. And my daughter can't wait to undergo it, because all her friends have already done it.

The young people undergoing the ritual feel pain, to be sure. But not as much as that endured by their parents, who must come up with big bucks so their children's teeth can be prodded, pushed, and pulled into positions deemed aesthetically pleasing to the tribal clan. Parents are willing to do this, even if it is a financial hardship, because they believe that their child will never enter middle-class America without artificially straightened teeth.

This ritual involves placing metal wire and brackets onto adolescent teeth that are then tightened every month until squeezed into the most desirable position. Sometimes, teeth must be pulled, in a horrific ceremony often accompanied by codeine and heavy drinking by the parent.

Family members assist, not only by selling their labor and cattle to pay for the procedure, but also by preparing soft, mushy foods for the day after each tightening episode, when the child's mouth is invariably sore.

The new thing of course now is for American children to get orthodontia twice, once while in grade school, and again later on, when they are starting to become obnoxious.

If you're an orthodontist, I'm sure you'll now be firing up your email account to write and tell me 8,037 reasons why nine-year-olds desperately need to wear braces. But I think it's a clever scheme designed primarily to extract more money from my wallet.

After all, two sets of braces foisted on the same kid (hold your breath here) cost a lot more than one set.

When Curly Girl was nine, I took her to the orthodontist associated with her dentist for a "free consultation." After the free consultation, they handed me a card with recommendations for two courses of braces, in the middle of which she was supposed to wear a retainer for two years.

After I woke up on the floor, recovering from my dead faint at the prices, I tried to imagine forcing my stubborn daughter to wear a mouthpiece every night for two years.

Really, the simpler thing would just be to move to

England, where they're still not so obsessed with cosmetic dentistry.

The interesting thing also is that no one at this orthodontist's office could give me any cogent reason why she needed two sets of braces. Except maybe that the orthodontist was buying a vacation home in Hawaii.

Proving once again what a bad mother I am, I skipped the whole nine-year-old braces thing and just told her she could have braces—after her brother's were done.

Well, I'm finished paying for Cheetah Boy's braces now, and bracing for the second round of bills for her dental work. No pun intended.

Curly Girl just had her "molds made," a procedure where they shove gooey stuff into your mouth to get an impression of your teeth. And she's eagerly awaiting the pain that's to come with the dental appliances, even though everyone's warned her how much it's going to hurt.

But then, kids will do anything to be just like their friends. And the amount of metal in the mouths of her middle-school friends right now could build a fighter jet, if it were all melted down for scrap.

So I'm counting my pennies and getting out the blender. It's time for the whipped carrots and sweet potatoes again.

## NOTHING EVER HAPPENS AT SCHOOL

I FEEL very sorry for my children. Now that they're in middle school, nothing ever happens to them anymore. Apparently, the tedium of their school days stretches out like a lifer in San Quentin, unrelieved by a single moment of joy, sadness or even a concert by Johnny Cash.

Consider this exchange that I had with fourteen-year-old Cheetah Boy:

Me: What did you do in school today?
Cheetah Boy: Nothing.
Me: I find that hard to believe, that nothing happened all
    day.
Cheetah Boy: Well, it's true.
Me: So you just sat there like a stone for seven hours?
Cheetah Boy: Pretty much.
Me: Did you see Travis? Is he over his flu?
Cheetah Boy: I don't know. He wasn't there.
Me: Did you play baseball at lunch? Who did you play with?
Cheetah Boy: I don't remember.
Me: I heard a flying saucer landed and took off with the en-
    tire third-period algebra class.
Cheetah Boy: Oh yeah? I missed it. I was in the bathroom.
Me: So did anyone get excited about that?
Cheetah Boy: No, not really. I'm hungry. Can I have a snack
    and go outside?

It has become clear that Cheetah Boy now greatly prefers interacting with total strangers on social media to spending twenty seconds talking to me. If I want to find out what is going on in his life, I generally have to go onto his Facebook page, though I will tell you this is no party at the beach.

If you think teenagers are monosyllabic in person, just try reading their social media accounts. No glittering prose there. No budding Mark Twains, Oscar Wildes or Jane Austens have yet manifested themselves in the set to which my children belong. What you read online is a mostly unrelenting version of what they text each other, which consists mostly of witty exchanges like, "'Sup?" and "Hey," enlivened by the occasional, "Wassssuuup lol."

Unlike her brother, Curly Girl still occasionally talks to me about what's going on in her life, since she's only twelve and hasn't yet been taken over completely by alien pods, but things are also changing rapidly on that front.

The girl who used to burst in the door full of news about her day also now has nothing to say. The little girl who used to beg me to spend time with her now goes into her room and closes her door with its new Yale locks that would make a Manhattan dweller proud.

Okay, she doesn't really have deadbolts on her door, but she'd have them if I would let her. I only know she's in there because I can hear the music playing.

I used to have a life before I had kids, or so I vaguely recall. It might be time to find it again, so I can have someone other than Buddy the Wonder Dog to talk to. Then, when the kids ask me what I've been doing, I can answer: "Nothing."

## DISNEYLAND, MINUS ONE

SOMETIMES an angel just lands on your shoulder.

That's what happened to me when I adopted Cheetah Boy and Curly Girl because their parents couldn't take care of them anymore. It's not that they're twins; in fact, they're two years apart. They certainly don't look alike, since they had fathers of different races. One is a boy, one is a girl. (At least I think so, since they're at the age now when they won't let me in while they're getting dressed.)

But they've been together through really hard times: when they were little and there was no food to eat in their house, then snatched away by well-meaning but brainless social workers and plunked into foster homes full of strangers, then into the house of a fat, frumpy middle-aged lady who became their new mom.

Through all of that, these kids show their closeness like couples everywhere, by bickering constantly. They still do almost everything together.

Recently, I was thinking back to the first time I took them to Disneyland, for Curly Girl's fourth birthday. This was shortly after they moved in and our adoption wasn't even final yet.

Now these were kids who'd never even been on an elevator or escalator before I met them. They'd never been in a swimming pool or been visited by Santa. So you can imagine their excitement about going to the legendary Magic Kingdom.

The morning of Curly Girl's birthday, I was awakened at four o'clock in the morning by a light turned on in the living room. I got up to investigate and walked in to find two small children sitting on the couch, completely dressed from head to toe. They were even wearing jackets and had tied their shoes.

"What are you doing?" I asked them, feeling just the tiniest bit irritable at being awakened from a sound sleep.

"We're waiting to go to Disneyland," they explained, looking at me as if this should have been obvious. They were quite crestfallen to be told to go back to bed.

That all came back to me recently on the morning of Curly Girl's eleventh birthday, as I sat trying to decide what to do.

My neighbor who works at Disneyland had offered to walk us in as guests, so we could go for free even though the park stopped offering its "get in for free on your birthday" deal. But it was a weekday, which meant taking the kids out of school.

I had no problem signing Curly Girl out early; she's always at the top of her class, having not yet been disillusioned by the American educational system. But this year Cheetah Boy has been struggling in school. He's smart as a whip, but lately he's always in trouble for acting like Larry, Curly or

Moe in class. Homework has also been a constant battle as he learns how to study. I've been on him like a cheap suit on this issue, since I don't want a son whose only career option is asking, "Do you want fries with that?" a hundred and fifty times a day.

I kept thinking it over, and I simply could not justify taking him out of school when I was just lecturing him about the poor quality of his work. At the same time, though, I couldn't imagine taking one half of this set to the Happiest Place on Earth while leaving the other one home. Would Curly Girl even have fun without her brother? Would Cheetah Boy be crushed to be left behind? Would he feel betrayed? Abandoned?

I spent half an hour furiously weighing the options.

And, sadly, I decided that Cheetah Boy had to stay behind. I just could not reward him for goofing off by giving him the day off from school, not to mention that he really needs every minute of classroom instruction these days. So I called him out of class when I picked up his sister and explained the situation. To my surprise, he got the message immediately, and only grimaced.

Curly Girl and I had fun at the park together, even though I'd covered too many accidents at Disneyland as a reporter, and I tend to scream fun things like, "Look out! Aieee! The track's coming loose!" and "I'm not sitting in the front row, that's the likeliest spot for a decapitation!" on all the rides.

Curly Girl was happy to pick all the rides herself, though she probably missed the familiar  non-stop bickering with her brother over which land to visit next. Since it was early January, the lines to everything were short or nonexistent.

After school, Cheetah Boy called every fifteen minutes to check on our progress. We updated him as we made our way around the park.

When we got back, late, Cheetah Boy had done all his

homework without prompting. This was roughly the equivalent of the Miracle at Lourdes.

And, for the next few weeks, he was much more motivated to do well in school.

I have no idea if the day he missed at Disneyland is the reason for his sudden desire to improve his work. But I feel good that, at least for once, I followed through on a consequence and didn't wimp out. For a few minutes at least, that made me the Happiest Mom on Earth.

## THE SPACE SHUTTLE IS QUIETER THAN MY KIDS

IF YOU'VE flown to Tokyo surrounded by crying babies, and you work in a freight train depot, and you operate a leaf blower ten hours a day, you're still not prepared for the sheer amount of noise you're going to face as a parent.

Really, they should require an environmental impact report on the noise pollution generated by your proposed child before the whole child-rearing project is even approved.

If you've ever gone to see a space shuttle land, accompanied by a Rolling Stones concert, with a NASCAR race in the background, that's now roughly the decibel level in my house on a daily basis.

And the problem is: You actually have to listen. You can't stick cotton in your ears and zone out, because the eleventh time the Precious One comes running up to you shrieking "MommyDaddyMommyDaddy" she might be telling you the house is on fire.

Of course, she probably just wants to tell you that the dog ate a bug. But you have to listen anyway, just in case.

When my kids were little, there was the delightful shouting, pounding, and bickering. Now that they're teens, it's the joyous sound of pounding techno pop and hip-hop booming from every room in the house.

I've always hated extraneous noise, being the kind of person who sought out the peace of wilderness on vacation and fantasized about shooting out the speakers on the ice-cream truck.

But being a parent does dull your auditory senses, just like it dumbs down your taste in movies to the point that *Karate Dog* takes on the aura of *Citizen Kane*.

"Can we go in the other room where the kids aren't making such a racket?" my friend who doesn't have kids asked me one day.

Racket? What racket? All I could hear was one drum set, a remote control car, and a tetherball being whacked at once, accompanied by a small amount of high-pitched squealing.

Some moms spend the day at a spa or go shopping to get away from this. I used to fantasize about an afternoon in a sensory deprivation tank. Though any parent will tell you the only time to worry is when the house gets too quiet.

That's when the enemy is getting ready to sabotage your mood. You're sweeping the hallway, whistling a happy tune, and then it suddenly occurs to you that you haven't heard any whooping, hollering, pounding, screeching, bouncing, shouting, giggling, bashing, crashing or wailing for a while.

Thwack! You turn a corner and discover the bathroom has been artistically redecorated with green and purple Sharpies.

Silence plus absent kids invariably means an "uh oh" moment is coming.

They're playing doctor in the closet. Or they've discovered the leftover spray paint in the garage.

Believe me, you'd rather have the former than the latter, which I can demonstrate if you come over and look at my patio.

And don't ask me about the candles lit under our cypress tree by a very quiet child. You could ask the fire department, though. They have a whole report on it.

So, yes, enjoy all that racket and fighting and snarling. It means, really, there's nothing wrong at all. After this happens a few times, you begin to dread silence as ominous. And, now that my kids are teens and regularly ditch me in favor of going to the mall with their friends, the strange silence in the house reminds me that this phase of motherhood is ending for me—a scary concept.

I'm glad when they come home and start blasting their music again, because it makes the house feel lived in, at least for a few nanoseconds before it makes my head pound.

Still, there's one annoying sound I know I'll never hear from my children: The vacuum cleaner. Thanks for sparing me, kids. We'll save that one for my clean-freak mom when she comes to visit.

## WARNING! ICEBERG AHEAD

THIS ISN'T something that occurs to you before you have kids, but afterward you know it all too well: When kids behave perfectly, something is deeply wrong.

The starship has been invaded by aliens. Their small bodies have been taken over by pods from outer space. Or maybe they just want something.

Bath towels not only can be located, but also seem to be hung up instead of lying in wet clumps on the floor. Smiling angelic miniature humans ask if they can get you anything while they're in the kitchen. Your teenager does not snarl when asked to unload the dishwasher. Your child mysteriously does not want to eat, even when you offer a cookie. A kid in your house turns off the TV, even when no one makes him. When renting a video, your offspring inquires, "Mom, what would you like to watch?"

Kids do not argue over whose turn it is to ride shotgun in the car. There's no battle over bedtime.

Your kid immediately comes home when you tell her to.

Personally, I ask no questions during these blips. I like to ride this horse until it gets tired. Soon enough, the end of the story will be revealed.

Your kid doesn't want a cookie because he already ate the contents of the cookie jar while you were taking a shower. She doesn't fight going to bed because she's got the flu. And she came straight home from her friend's house because they spent all afternoon painting her mom's mirror with fingernail polish, and she knows the hour of revelation is nearly at hand. Your teenager who doesn't snarl at chores wants to borrow the car. And the kid who offers you something from the kitchen is about to ask if she can go to Disneyland for her birthday. With six friends.

## I'M FLUNKING THE SEVENTH GRADE

I DIDN'T fail the seventh grade when I was twelve years old, and I certainly never thought I would have to live through it all again. But that was before I had a twelve-year-old kid who seems determined to give me a stroke before he can grow up, or at least drive me into a lunatic asylum.

Cheetah Boy is a really, really smart kid. But he has been so scatterbrained with his work this year that I finally took over with personal supervision. I started forcing him to sit down with me every day after school and go over everything he did in class that day, including reviewing his homework and any assignments due the following day.

He's not really in favor of this process.

At first, he indicated his disapproval by refusing and pitching giant fits. There was a lot of screaming and yelling on both our sides as I insisted that—as God is my witness— he would be passing the seventh grade. Eventually, after a few days, he stopped at least the most vigorous complaining. There is still some passive resistance, but we've made progress.

Fortunately, he's good in math, since I could not do his seventh-grade algebra to save my life. I couldn't do seventh-grade algebra when I was actually in seventh grade. I certainly can't do it now.

News flash: We interrupt this story to record the phone call I just received from Cheetah Boy at 8:52 in the morning: "Hey Mom, I forgot my planner, can you bring it to school for me?"

No, sorry dude, I don't fetch and carry things that kids forgot. Thanks for proving my point, though, about how scatterbrained you have become. Yesterday he forgot his school badge and had to sit at detention for lunch. Now, back to your regularly scheduled column.

The thing that's really annoying, though, about all this studying is that I looked online yesterday at Cheetah Boy's grades, posted on the School Loop website every day, and we have an "F" in English!

He failed to turn in an important essay that comprised a huge amount of his grade, one that I know he worked on and that he assured me was turned in.

He also got forty-eight out of seventy-two on his cluster test—a test that we studied hard for on Sunday afternoon and restudied again Monday morning, a test that he knew every answer to when he walked out the door on Monday. So how on earth could he have done so poorly?

After I finished yelling at him about the "F" and telling him he's grounded from TV and computers, and grounded to the yard until that "F" comes up to a "B," he managed to find the assignment he was supposed to turn in.

It was under the couch.

God help us all.

I wasn't too crazy about going through seventh grade and I don't like reliving it, either. But if I have to live it again with him, then WE WILL NOT BE FLUNKING.

Why can't he be more like his sister? Curly Girl loves school and gets straight A's. Meanwhile, I'll be guzzling some of the Sauza Gold tequila I bought at Albertsons on sale for $5.99.

As Bartles and Jaymes said, thank you for your support.

## LITTERING REALLY BUGS ME

I RECENTLY conducted an Extremely Scientific Survey of 1,848 teenage kids, all of whom were crammed into my son's bedroom at the time. I asked them to identify the best thing to do with a wrapper once its contents have been removed. Examples cited were empty Doritos bags, plastic water bottles, In-N-Out hamburger wrappers, McDonald's shake cups, and the like.

Here is a tally of their responses:

1,791 kids said you should "drop it on the floor."

Forty-eight kids said you should "drop it onto the nearest available surface."

Six kids said you should "put it in the trash but only when your mom is looking."

One kid said you should "light it on fire and see if it'll burn." (That child is now banned from my house).

Two kids said you should "always put it in the trash receptacle."

Now, you understand, I didn't actually see those last two

kids. They were in the back of the room, and any evidence they exist may have been retouched, like those photos of the Loch Ness Monster.

I would, however, like to believe that they are real. Sort of like I hope that there are politicians who don't lie and my bank really does care about me when I'm on hold.

For any foreigners reading this, I would like to explain that these are average American suburban kids, who actually are probably familiar with the concept of a trash can and have likely seen many in their lives.

If we were in Switzerland, things would be different, because that is a country so obsessed with cleanliness that their highways are cleaner than my dining room table. I was in Lucerne once when it was snowing, where shopkeepers were so outraged that snowflakes were defiling their sidewalks that they were out there sweeping them off while flakes were still falling.

I can only imagine what would happen to a teenager there who dared to drop a Twinkies wrapper on the ground. They might sit him down and force him to listen to yodeling for twenty-four consecutive hours, or eat nothing but fondue.

Here in America, though, I don't know how much upbringing contributes to this teenage interest in decorating our fine nation with potato chip bags and Ho Ho wrappers.

I have nagged my children continuously for ten years about using the trash can, with only limited results. I recently decided the only thing to do is stop buying things that come in wrappers. It's healthier to eat fresh food anyway, not to mention cheaper, so no more $200 trips to Costco, thank you very much.

There are still times, though, when we have to eat on the go.

In my antique Toyota 4Runner, my kids just fling things

into the back trunk area. If they fall behind the soccer chairs and beach blankets that live there permanently, I can go a year without finding them. Unless it's an orange I have given them to eat. Then it will eventually make its aromatic presence known.

This continues to be a vexing problem of great scientific interest to me, and probably too many parents out there. The study I mentioned was conducted with a grant from the Parents Are Not Too Stupid (PANTS) organization that I founded. . . .

## IS SCHOOL MORE THAN PE?

IT'S TIME for students to pick their elective courses for next year, and let's just say that my son and I don't see eye-to-eye about what he should study in the eighth grade. If Cheetah Boy had his druthers, eighth grade would consist of four daily PE classes, plus one section as a teacher's aide for PE, plus learning to speak Italian.

I feel he doesn't really need to speak Italian until he buys me a house in Tuscany, which is probably not going to happen for at least ten years.

I know, I know. Some of you think I should let him choose his own electives, but it's just not going to happen. He's going to learn Spanish, so he can speak to my neighbors when I retire to Puerto Vallarta.

You may notice that I haven't mentioned Curly Girl yet, even though she's going off to sixth grade middle school next year. That's because we agreed in about thirty seconds that she should take chorus, art, and marine biology. So far, we're in perfect harmony.

Sigh, if only her brother weren't such a boy.

**My idea of a good schedule for Cheetah Boy:**
- Really Hard Algebra That Mom Doesn't Have to Help Him With
- English Literature and Composition
- Cooking for Fun and Profit
- The Art of Hanging the Bathroom Towel
- How to Remove Germs from Household Surfaces
- Why You Shouldn't Waste All Your Money on Junk Food
- One Hundred Reasons to Never Get a Motorcycle
- Ways to Fix Mom's Computer When It Goes on the Fritz

**Cheetah Boy's idea of a good schedule:**
- Algebra for Athletes, aka Who Cares, the Game Is Friday
- How to Text in Class Without Getting Your Phone Taken Away
- The Comic Book as Literature: The Garfield Years
- Driver Education for Adolescents
- Italian for People Who Like Pizza
- Baseball Practice for Extreme Jocks
- Creative Video Gaming
- Ways to Use Mom's Computer to Watch Goopy Music Videos

Is there any room for compromise? I guess time will tell on that one.

## I'M DREAMING OF A FAKE CHRISTMAS

IT'S DECEMBER again, and our family is debating a topic we revisit every year. Not paper or plastic. Not "Merry

Christmas" or "Happy Holidays." Not even whether to send out Christmas cards with newsletters that deceive. (Johnny is enjoying his wonderful new campus, omitting to mention that it's a minimum-security prison, not UCLA.)

Our debate every year is over whether to get a real Christmas tree or a fake one.

When I was a youngster, I was always firmly on the "real tree" side of the Mason-Dixon Line. Real trees smell better. They look better, at least until December 28th or so. And, dare I say it, they're real. I don't dispute any of this. But that, of course, was because I was a kid.

Kids don't have to buy the trees. They don't have to tie them to the tops of their cars. They don't have to clean up the billion pounds of pine needles that drop all over the floor every minute. They don't have to untangle dusty strings of lights to adorn them. And they don't have to take them down, dragging another one million pine needles along with them as they reluctantly leave the house.

For several years I have been a single mom, which is synonymous with "person who has way too much to do every second of the day." As a result, I've reluctantly joined the fake tree camp, especially now that they're making them with built-in lights. We don't have a fake tree yet, but people can dream, can't they?

Let me explain: Before I adopted my adorable children, I used to have fantasies of the wonderful times we'd have decorating our Christmas tree together as a family. We'd make popcorn and construction paper garlands and hang them, while drinking hot chocolate and watching *It's a Wonderful Life*. We'd be wearing colorful Christmas sweaters with cute sayings on them, and maybe someone would don a Santa hat as he carefully unpacked the special Christmas ornaments we bought every year and treasured. Everyone would ooh and aah. Christmas carols would play in the background, and maybe we couldn't help but join in the singing.

That was my best guess as to how our Christmas tree rituals would play out every year. And then I woke up.

For the past two years, we've been so busy every minute that I neglected the trip to buy a tree until a few days before Christmas. Finally, the kids would say, "Mommy! We have to go get the tree!" And I would agree, we'd all jump in the car, and drive around fruitlessly for miles, trying to find a lot that still had a tree left.

Last year (and as Dave Barry says, I am not making this up), Curly Girl was almost in tears when we arrived at our familiar cheapskate lot—where I drive miles out of the way because I refuse to pay $35 for a tree—and they were taking down the tents.

"Oh, no, Mommy, it's closed," she began to wail. But as we looked harder, we realized there was one tree. One lonely tree left on the lot, as the workmen dismantled the pipes holding up the tent.

"Hold on," I told Curly Girl. "We're going to get it." And I zoomed into the lot, while she threw herself headlong out of the car and rushed up to the workmen, begging them to sell us the tree.

A great shout of victory rose up from the vicinity of my 1997 4Runner, as the last guy on the last lot agreed to take $20 for the last tree, and tied it to the top of my car.

When we got home, there was no time to waste. We only had an hour or so to decorate the tree, because the kids had parties to go to, and homework to do, and practice for the church Christmas pageant.

We flung the ornaments on the tree—at least Curly Girl and I did. I snarled at the kids not to hang anything until I untangled the bleeping lights and got them hung first. Cheetah Boy has no patience for tree decoration, and only likes to fling handfuls of tinsel icicles that get all over the floor and are always in danger of being eaten by the dog.

A few ornaments got broken along the way, and a string of lights went out, and then there was an emergency trip to the store to get more lights, and some artistic bickering over design elements and more bickering over who was going to sweep up all the pine needles and the tinsel on the floor before the dog ate it, and then it was done.

No hot chocolate. No popcorn garlands. I turned to look for Cheetah Boy and he had already gone outside to play baseball.

So that was last year's saga, and it was pretty similar to the previous year, and the year before that. For this reason, I can't really see why our tradition can't incorporate a plastic tree, considering it's already sharply abbreviated. Yet the kids find this idea as heinous as if I suggested a Styrofoam birthday cake.

Right now, I'm on the fence on this topic. Though I can think of at least one good reason to get a real tree: At least you have to take it down at some point. Over the years, I've been in quite a few houses where people never bothered to take down their Christmas trees. I'm sorry, but it just looks weird.

I haven't sunk that low. At least not yet. Though don't ask me about the plastic bin of Christmas lights or how they never quite made it out to the garage until they were needed again this year.

## IN THE BATTLE OVER FALLING PANTS, I'VE BUCKLED

LATE AT night, I like to gather my children around me and tell them stories from the old days, back when guys wore belts to hold up their pants.

I have to explain the concept of belts, of course, and that pants also used to fit around the waist, which prevented them from sliding down guys' hips until they reached the Earth's molten core. Nowadays, as our eleven-year-old friend Nico explains, boys must keep their hands in their pockets at all times to hold up their pants, since they are no longer fitted and belts can be found only in museums.

This has its advantages. Boys with their hands permanently immobilized in their pockets can't wipe grimy paws on my clean towels. They can't smack their sisters nor leave a dirty palm print on the wall.

Over the past year, Cheetah Boy's pants have fallen lower and lower on his hips, as if he were some poor starvation victim whose clothes are hanging off him. But, of course, all that's happening is that he is refusing to wear any bottoms that don't display the tops of his boxers.

This just shows how much impact I've had on my kid's thinking. For years, I used to constantly point out "fashion victims," guys who were so obsessed with this gangster style that their pants actually fell down, or who had to hold their crotch as they ran, lest they trip over their falling pants and go head over heels.

Back in those days, we would all laugh at how silly these guys were, and how pathetic that they would allow their need to be trendy to interfere with the actual functioning of their lives.

When Cheetah Boy, now fourteen, first started letting his underwear show, I fought back.

We had Normandy-sized battles over his need to show plaid—i.e., the plaid designs of his cotton boxer shorts. Eventually, though, he wore me down with his persistent refusal to follow my rules.

So I gave up.

Amazingly, my surrender in the Battle of the Droopy

Drawers became a clever strategy, instead of pathetic weakness. I read a slew of books about parenting teenagers, all of which advised me to pick my battles, and not to get into power struggles over fashion statements. As long as my son is getting decent grades and has good behavior in other ways, I just decided not to care how ridiculous he looks.

Some of my friends have been shocked by this, as if I have suddenly become a traitor to parenthood itself. Maybe in their minds, I should be thrown in the stocks and flogged for high crimes and treason against other moms and dads.

"But Marla, this style started in prison. Because the guys can't wear belts in there. It's a prison style," one friend argued. But as long as my kid is not in prison, I don't much care.

Even the cafeteria lady at school was laughing at Cheetah Boy and singing "Pants on the ground" to him one day when they were particularly egregious, according to his sister, a reliable witness.

But when I start questioning my decision, I remember what I wore when I was a teenager.

The skirts that were so ridiculously short that, if I dropped a pencil, I had to just keep walking, because there was no way I could pick it up without flashing everyone behind me.

The white lipstick that made me look like a corpse. The boyfriends with shaggy hair that drove their parents insane. The hot pants.

Oh, lord.

The hot pants.

Hmm. Suddenly the low-rider shorts don't seem so bad after all.

## TEN THINGS MY TEENS CAN'T DO

MY TEENAGE children can disassemble any electronic device and put it back together in nanoseconds.

They can instantly provide convincing arguments as to how the dog got into the refrigerator and ate the chocolate pie I was saving for dessert. They can explain to me how the webcam on my computer works.

What they can't do is put toilet paper onto the roller in the bathroom.

This advanced mechanical skill has apparently eluded them, despite the fact that they mastered cold fusion in their bedrooms just last week.

I judge this from the fact that the past 870 times I walked into their bathroom, there was no toilet paper on the roll. There is plenty of bathroom tissue in that room—a veritable mountain of the stuff, in fact. I went to Costco the week before and bought one of those 900-roll bundles that takes up half your bathroom's square footage just to store it.

So the only explanation is that they simply don't know how to put it on the roll, right?

I'm not really sure what they're doing in place of using toilet paper, and, honestly, I don't want to know. I also don't want to know what's in their bedrooms, so I try to avoid walking in there unless absolutely necessary. I'm sure this makes me a very, very bad mother indeed, because, after all, there could be animals or even people living back there and I'd never know it. Sounds like the start of a movie where the creature comes to life in the children's bedroom, but the parents never even notice because they ludicrously don't go near it.

That would be me, Ms. Ludicrous.

Meanwhile, Cheetah Boy, who has instantly figured out how to work the TV remote in hotel rooms on four continents, doesn't know how to operate a broom. He explains this to me every week, when I assign him to sweep the floor. He also has very bad eyesight and can't see clods of dirt that he sweeps carefully around.

Cheetah Boy is already making preparation for his driver's training class two years from now. But if I were creating a class, it would include the following skills, which my children have never mastered, despite repeated lessons:

1. How to put a roll of toilet paper on the bathroom roller
2. How to scrub a pot so the food inside is removed
3. How to operate a broom
4. How to dry your clothes without removing your mother's damp laundry from the clothes dryer first
5. How to remove soap scum from a sink
6. How to flush a toilet
7. How to empty a trash can
8. How to tell when the dog's bowl is empty
9. How to close the refrigerator door
10. How to fold cereal bags so the cereal inside stays fresh.

At least they know how to fix my computer when it breaks. And they're very good at eating. Especially shrimp and steak. Too bad they can't remember how to rinse the plates.

## NO MORE MAID, I'M BACK TO MOM

RECENTLY I had a minor nervous breakdown, during which I decided I was completely over my kids. The thrill was gone. I wanted a divorce.

I'm sure you've never felt that way, but I decided that being the mom of teenagers wasn't nearly as much fun as everyone promised me it would be.

It all started innocently, when I took Curly Girl and

three of her adolescent girlfriends overnight to San Diego for her thirteenth birthday. She had begged to do this, and in a fit of dementia, I thought it would be a great idea. Next time, I'm just going to bash a brick into my skull for twenty-eight hours. It will be cheaper and more fun.

During the trip, the four girls treated me like the maid— or maybe the nanny—since I not only cleaned up after them but also paid for everything. And I came back fuming—so angry I made them listen to Broadway musicals in the car all the way home.

I got home, in what could be only described as a sour mood, and discovered that Cheetah Boy, who spent the previous night with a friend, had invited a whole bunch of high-school kids over to our house for a party that very night.

Yes, I know, that sounds like a mother's dream of heaven. Hordes of adolescents tromping through the house eating everything like a biblical plague of locusts.

Regardless, I snapped and made everyone go home. There may have been some yelling involved. I don't really remember. It's all a blur.

That was the point at which I just decided I wasn't going to be a mom anymore.

I was done cooking and cleaning for monosyllabic teenagers who flinched when I touched them and grumbled when I tried to shove delicious home-cooked meals down their throats, before sneaking over to McDonalds to eat garbage. I decided that, from now on, I would just provide them with shelter and a refrigerator full of food. For everything else, they were on their own.

Ergo, I stopped cooking and cleaning and just lay on the couch with an adult beverage in my hand, watching—for once—the shows I liked on TV. Any question the kids asked me was answered with a mumbled, "Dunno."

This went on for a couple of days before it seemed to

sink in that I really was no longer Mom, a.k.a. Maid Marla, the lady who nags you to eat your vegetables. This may have happened when I was chopping onions and crying in the kitchen for a dinner I was making for myself alone.

"I noticed you've been in a really bad mood lately," Cheetah Boy finally said. "Is anything wrong?"

"No, everything's just fine," I snapped, wondering if an adolescent was capable of grasping sarcasm. Then, I realized with horror that I was acting exactly like my own passive-aggressive family, in which every emotional scene turned into *The Price Is Right*, during which the participants were supposed to guess how the other is feeling.

So I told him that I was very sad because I didn't feel like we were a family any more, that all he and his sister did was text their friends every minute and ignore me, and our house was just a way station to change clothes. And that I missed the days when they were cute little kids and we all did things together.

Greatly to my astonishment, he said he felt the same way. He said that every time he tried to pour out his heart to his sister, she turned away and started texting in the middle of the conversation.

"Imagine if you had two people doing that to you," I told him. "All the time. Would you like it?"

No, he said, he wouldn't. And then he told me that he thought technology was ruining our family life. And he vowed to turn off the TV and spend more time with the family.

We had rather a long talk, remarkable because I thought he had lost the power of speech in eighth grade. I really could not believe the wise and insightful things that were coming out of his fourteen-year-old mouth.

I started feeling a little more cheerful. The very next day, when I proposed taking Buddy the Wonder Dog to the dog beach together, the kids piled in the car without even once complaining that the trip was ruining their lives.

At the dog beach, the kids—without speaking—locked their phones in the glove box and actually went to the beach free of electronics, something that hasn't happened since, well, ever.

I couldn't help wondering if some aliens had perchance come down and kidnapped my real kids and replaced them with these pleasant avatars. I was thinking that, if so, I really didn't mind.

At bedtime that night, Curly Girl even kissed me goodnight. And I decided that maybe I wouldn't mind being their mom for at least a couple more days.

But I'm keeping the TV remote and the adult beverages nearby, just in case.

## HORRORS! THE TEACHER TOOK AWAY THE CELL PHONE!

I WAS working at home the other morning when I got a deeply outraged phone call from Cheetah Boy, who was between classes in school. Apparently, a despotic teacher unfairly took away his cellphone in class, even though he absolutely was not texting or doing anything inappropriate with it at all.

In fact, the phone just happened to fall out of his pocket, where it wasn't even turned on, and while he was in the process of innocently putting it back into his pocket, it turned itself on and made a noise, at which point the teacher swooped in and confiscated it, even though it clearly was not his fault.

This was just so wrong and so unfair in so many ways, my son explained to me. So could I please go that very afternoon and pick it up from impound at the office, so he could have it back?

In one respect, I was actually happy to get this phone call, because the high school's previous policy was that teachers confiscated phones if they saw them in class, and that kids then had to pay $5 in the office to get them back.

I didn't like this, because I'd overheard boys laughing and boasting that their parents wouldn't ever have to find out their phones had been jacked, because they merely had to go to the office themselves and pay $5 to redeem them. So I was glad to hear it had been changed, and I would be notified in the unlikely case that my child ever broke this rule.

Yet I felt an ocean of sympathy for my teenage son, for the unjust and potentially life-threatening deprivation he was facing, especially because he had left for school that morning without forgetting any of his homework or hollering at anyone, even once.

See, my kids can't conceive of living a single, solitary second without a phone attached somewhere to their persons. If they could have it surgically implanted, they'd be signing up for the procedure now.

I try to explain to them about the olden days, when Tyrannosaurus Rex was king, I spent my entire childhood and most of my adult life without ever using a mobile phone. When ordinary people could go the entire day without calling someone. When the idea of sending text messages or taking pictures with your phone wasn't even science fiction, because no one had thought of it yet.

This is no more comprehensible to them than the idea of Hannibal's army crossing the Alps on elephants.

Once or twice a year, I deliberately take them to places where there's no phone reception, such as Big Sur or rural Alaska. This doesn't really break their dependence, but at least they learn they won't actually die if they can't text "Sup?" 2,000 times a day to everyone they've ever met.

I considered whether to agree to Cheetah Boy's frantic begging, leave my work and drive over to his school to fetch his phone. In fact, I even asked the fans on my Facebook page what to do. Do not get it, they all advised.

Since I always do what people on the internet tell me, I decided I was much too busy, and left it until the next day.

When he got home, Cheetah Boy was disappointed but not obnoxious when I told him I'd been too busy to make it over there. The next morning, I did take pity on him and accompanied him to high school to retrieve his phone. Well, accompany is the wrong word, because it implies we were walking together. In fact, he was walking ten feet in front of me, because if he is ever seen near school walking with his mother, the Earth would open up and swallow him forever.

He did—by coincidence, though—happen to be in the office at the same time I was, enabling him to accept the phone when it was released from the hoosegow and promise the school secretary it wouldn't happen again.

"Darn right it won't happen again," I told her, glaring at my son. He just looked away and studied the acoustic ceiling tiles as if he were going to have a test on them.

Driving home, I thought back to the last time I misplaced my own phone. Yikes. I was just as frantic—am I turning into a teenager?

## RECONSIDERING *GRAND THEFT AUTO*

BECAUSE I am an extremely weak-willed person and bad mother in general, I violated my own vow to myself and bought my son a video game system. I know a lot of you are probably shrugging your shoulders and thinking, "So what?" because your family has been playing these games for years.

But I was determined that Cheetah Boy would not rot

his brain on such trash.

Instead, he would spend his leisure hours as a teenager in uplifting activities, such as reading *War and Peace*, raising money for starving children or maybe composing a new Mozart opera.

I even wrote a column about this a few years ago titled "Video Games Were Invented by the Devil." I followed it up with "My Bad: Video Games Are not from Satan," in which I explained that they were created by Voldemort.

This was all intended to be funny, but obsessed gamers worldwide took it seriously enough to send me some eight hundred hate comments and even death threats, including that I should be burned to death or fall into a hole and die and then be burned to death. The video-gaming community really has no sense of irony.

And it certainly is ironic that I—the last holdout parent in the known galaxy—should finally break down and purchase my son an Xbox 360.

I did it mostly so I could take it away from him, using it as a consequence for undesirable behavior. And it has worked for that purpose. But little did I know that his video gaming would teach some important life lessons, especially *Grand Theft Auto*, which his friends bring over and play when I'm not around.

As we have discussed, *Grand Theft Auto* is the hugely popular video game series in which players portray urban criminals who commit crimes, steal cars, and then run from the cops—a realistic scenario in which they encounter prostitutes, drug dealers, mob kingpins, and other upstanding individuals who provide role models for America's youth.

This game has been around for years and spawned numerous editions, so kids have a chance to get involved in a wide variety of underworld assignments, and rehearse their future roles as assassins, cocaine dealers, and more.

Unlike the mom a few years ago who called the cops because her son would not stop playing *Grand Theft Auto*, I have been impressed by some of the things my son has learned while playing this game, like these inspirational life lessons:

- If you shoot a cop, and then hide for five minutes, everyone will forget all about it.
- You can carry a sniper rifle, a chainsaw, a pistol, machine gun, and grenades in your pocket, all at the same time.
- Beware because, during a heist, your girlfriend might shoot you.
- You can be killed and come back to life, even if you don't believe in Jesus.
- If you run over people during a high-speed chase, they aren't killed, but only knocked out for a bit.
- If you're being chased by the police, get a different-colored car. They'll never catch you.
- Bald men can go into a barber shop and come out with an Afro.
- By painting your car, you can fix all the damage.

And, according to a recent news report, kids can even learn to drive: A six-year-old boy in Virginia told police he had learned to drive by playing *Grand Theft Auto*, which is why he managed to drive his mom's car ten miles before striking a utility pole. Sadly, unlike the video game, the car didn't manage to fix itself and keep going. Thankfully, though, the boy wasn't hurt, though he was somewhat miffed that sheriff's deputies wouldn't let him walk the rest of the way to school.

These are only a few of the things that kids can learn from this game, which is rated "Mature" for adults only. Of course, the "Mature" rating to kids means, "Play your older brother's or dad's copy because your mom won't let you buy it."

Personally, I'd like to see *Grand Theft Auto: Incarceration*, in which the criminals will all be doing time in maximum-security prisons, surrounded by cold-hearted prison guards and sharpshooters in high towers, after all their victims come and testify against them at trial. Until then, we'll just have to content ourselves with the lessons we've already learned.

## IN HOT WATER AGAIN

I NEVER scold my kids by telling them they're in hot water because, well, they'd like that. Now that they're teenagers, I realize I spent the first half of their lives coaxing them into the shower, and the second half trying to get them out.

When they were little, I used to fret that they'd turn into big, round, smelly clods of dirt that would just roll down the street, because it was so hard to get them into the bathtub. Friends with older children told me, "Don't worry. When they discover the opposite sex, that problem will disappear."

And, now, sure enough, my anxiety over their personal hygiene has gone down to the exact proportion that my hot water bill has gone up.

"Seriously. Get out of the shower. Now," is the most common phrase uttered around my house these days. Followed by, "I'm not kidding. Get out."

If I let him, Cheetah Boy would spend $800 a week on Axe shower products that are so smelly, the toxic-waste people come to my house asking if I'm manufacturing methamphetamine here. I just point to the bathroom and mention that I have a teenage boy, and they smile sympathetically and move on.

Curly Girl is also a hot water aficionado and requires a variety of costly personal care products to augment the steam. I've considered various methods of cutting the hot water bill, including turning down the water heater. Unfortunately, that means that I, the wage earner, also have to take short showers, which is not hugely appealing on any level.

We only have one shower in our house for three of us to share. I know that's un-American, but sue me. That's all we can afford.

Maybe I can install a pay system like they have at state park campgrounds, where you must put in quarters to get a few minutes of hot water. I never knew how fast I could wash my hair until I had to pump in quarter after quarter for what seemed like mere nanoseconds of warm flow.

I once stayed in a cabin that had some sort of device that simply shut off the hot water after a few minutes—without warning—leaving you standing there with icy water cascading down onto a head full of suds. That was certainly effective, but it might spark a rebellion if installed at Chez Frumpy.

My friend Theresa told me she used to go outside and turn off the water main to the house, as a last resort. A great example of thinking outside the box. Of course, that would require me to actually know where the water shutoff valve is located. I've only lived here six years, so that's not really enough time to have learned all these petty homeowner details.

Until I devise a solution, I'll just keep pounding on the bathroom door. That does work. Eventually. And my upper arms get some exercise, too.

## MY SON'S EARRINGS
## ARE A SIGHT FOR SORE EARS

WHEN Cheetah Boy turned eighteen, his first act as a legal

adult was to run away and join the circus.

No, just kidding, he didn't run away. Now that he's attained his majority, he just did something he's been threatening to do for years: He got both of his ears pierced. And, to add insult to injury, he put big fake rhinestone studs in them that almost seem to glow in the dark. They make my otherwise handsome son look like a cheesy wannabe hip-hop star. And, by the way, I don't mean rhinestones that are fake diamonds. I mean fake rhinestones. The faux following the faux.

The day after his birthday dinner, he came home with these headlights in his ears, glowing with pride and defiance. He couldn't wait for me to see them.

I made him happy by yelling when I saw them because I'd banned him from getting a pair of earrings for years. I knew he was waiting for the outburst, so I didn't want to disappoint him, but secretly I thought they wouldn't be so bad if they were just small gold studs or hoops.

The 8,072 parenting books I've read since my kids were little all advised me to ignore grooming issues on the theory that you should "pick your battles" and only throw a hissy over things that really matter. Your kid comes home with blue hair? Cool. Dye yours to match. Just make sure he still does his homework. Because it's really the homework you care about, right? Because the blue hair will probably disappear of its own accord if you ignore it.

The irony is that I wouldn't have minded if he'd only gotten one ear pierced, like the guys of my generation. I'd tried to help him get one ear pierced when we happened to be in San Francisco's Haight-Ashbury district on his sixteenth birthday. I thought it would be a great way to remember his first visit to the Haight. He'd been asking to get an ear pierced for a while.

Unfortunately, all the tattoo shops we visited required

proof of age before they'd stick any needles in, and he didn't have any with him. So he came home with earlobes intactus.

But that condition still bothered him. After he started playing football, he began agitating to get earrings in both ears.

"No," I told him. "It would make you look like a thug."

"My football coach has them," my son insisted. "So do all the players in the NFL."

"I don't care," I told him. "They look trashy."

Perhaps I was just making distinctions that seem arbitrary to the teenage mind, but the double-ear piercing look has always seemed the province of disreputable types and rappers who act and sound like they're from Compton even though they grew up in Woodland Hills.

Or as my kids would say, it's "ratchet."

Ratchet is a somewhat fluid slang expression that once meant a trashy, slutty woman but has since morphed into all things vaguely lawless and tasteless.

Reminds me of my own teenage years, to be sure, and the first few years I worked in Hollywood. But no need to mention any of that to the offspring.

In my distress over my son's new ratchet earlobes, I turned for sympathy to my teenage daughter, who often agrees with me over the general issue of whether her brother is a moron.

"Don't you think those earrings look hideous?" I asked Curly Girl, needing some reassurance.

She looked at me and rolled her eyes. "No."

"What are you talking about? They're awful," I continued, even as it began to dawn on me that I wasn't going to get any backup here.

"Mom, every guy at school is wearing earrings like that," she told me.

"What, they're all Liza Minnelli impersonators?" I asked.

She looked at me quizzically, and I realized she no more had any idea who Liza Minnelli was than I did Wiz Khalifa.

I also realized that my son used the money I had given him as a birthday present to get the ears pierced and buy the earrings I detested, which seemed wrong on so many levels that it short-circuited my brain to think about it.

Still, I'm trying to think positively about the whole situation. I guess I can be grateful that it was only his ears that were pierced. And at least they weren't a tattoo, or plugs.

The first night he brought them home, he came into my bathroom with the special ear cleaning solution he'd spent untold money to buy—when we have three bottles of peroxide that would work just as well—and asked me to come and help him clean his piercings.

"No, thanks," I told him. "I'd rather not."

"What?" he asked me, outraged that I wouldn't help him with his medical needs. "Why not?"

"Don't want to," I answered and turned the page on the book I was reading. He shook his head at this sign of maternal neglect and started working with the disinfectant himself.

I realized then that I do have some hope. If he keeps his ears as clean as he keeps his bedroom, they're bound to get infected. I'm not wishing infection on my son, but if it did happen, he'd have to take the earrings out until they healed.

Hmm. Then it's possible they could just disappear. Things disappear around our house all the time. It certainly would have nothing to do with me.


## PROM DRAMA, NEW AND UPDATED

I KNOW this will come as a surprise to you, but I haven't attended a high school prom in forty-two years.

Everyone who survived knows the misery of prom. Even if yours wasn't miserable, your friends' probably were. As I explained to my teenagers, "Don't expect to have fun and you'll be fine. It's really just a ritual you must endure in uncomfortable fancy clothes. And, if you have a good time, that's just a bonus."

My kids' proms were the first time I was doing it in stereo.

I did want Cheetah Boy to experience his prom. To that end, I paid a vast sum of money for prom tickets—more than the cost of tuition for my first quarter at university. Seriously. Not making that up. Meanwhile, his sister, who at the time was only a sophomore, was asked to the prom for the second year in a row. This time by her new boyfriend, who goes to a different high school.

Now, if you haven't been to a prom for a few decades, you wouldn't believe the paperwork that's involved. Yes, I said paperwork.

In my day, back when Triceratops roamed the earth, proms were held in the high school gym. Underclassmen would get together and spend countless hours decorating it for the seniors, who were the stars of the event.

But since then, there's been Promflation. Nowadays, proms are usually held in featureless hotel ballrooms, which might have hosted a real-estate-flipper's seminar that very afternoon and will host a wedding the next day.

I went to prom in a borrowed Camaro. Today, kids pool their money and hire limousines fancier than the one that President Nixon took to China. I know this for a fact, because I've seen it at the Nixon library.

If Promflation continues at its current rate, teens will probably be arriving by helicopter next year.

And, then, there are the ticket prices. Prom tickets at our school cost $100 if you waited until the last minute.

But you couldn't just walk up and buy a ticket. No siree. Students had to fill out a stack of paperwork that would have gladdened the hearts of bureaucrats in the Cold War Soviet Union. It's easier to get a job at the TSA than to get permission to go to a formal dance at our school.

After the kids fill out all the paperwork, they have to get it signed off by teachers and administrators, certifying they aren't serial killers, they turned in all their library books and won't vomit in the punch bowl.

My son, who had a demerit on his record, had to work for a teacher for an hour to get it cleared.

This caused a problem for Curly Girl. For complicated reasons, she didn't get all her paperwork done to attend prom at this other school. Plus, she and her boyfriend broke up.

After I gnashed my teeth and contemplated all the money I'd spent on The Dress and The Shoes for the big event, I managed to bite my lip, though it required choking down a lot of unnecessary chocolate.

However, the ex-boyfriend announced that his dad was giving him money for them to go out to dinner Saturday night in splendid style anyway, so they'd have their own mini-prom, regardless. He even found a date for my daughter's BFF, so they could double.

Meanwhile, my somewhat feckless son couldn't really decide what he wanted to do about his senior prom. I'd bought him the tickets, but then the hot college girl he planned to bring bailed out on him.

He vacillated, finally asking another girl. She already had plans to go with her girlfriends but told him to look for her there, and she'd dance with him.

So he decided to go stag. Then, a friend offered to let him ride in his limo. At the last minute, I rented him a tuxedo that also cost more than the downpayment on my house. I just refused to think about it.

Saturday was The Big Day, and my daughter went to her friend's house early to spend the day primping. Her date was picking her up at five thirty, she said.

"You'd better come over so I can take pictures," I warned her. "I spent a lot of money on that dress."

In the late afternoon my son donned his all-white tuxedo. He looked very handsome, though slightly like one of those fellows in white who stands outside supermarkets collecting for medical relief. I didn't mention that to him.

At five o'clock I dropped Cheetah Boy off near the home of his friend, where apparently parents were holding a pre-party before the kids got into the limo. I didn't know this family, but my kid is now eighteen, and I figure if he's old enough to join the Army and vote, he's old enough to get into a car with people I don't know.

Then, I called my daughter, only to find her sobbing. Apparently, the ex-boyfriend had texted her the following message: "I canceled the reservations. Don't ever call or text me again."

Needless to say, she was upset. But he refused to answer his phone to explain what was going on. She and her friend had already finished crying their eyes out, and were now regrouping.

I suggested we go to the ex-boyfriend's house and confront him. She was horrified.

"No! I'm over him! I just want to move on." The girls decided to dress up anyway, go out to a nice dinner and then wander around the mall, looking gorgeous and breaking the hearts of random males.

I drove to her friend's house to pick them up and chauffeur them to the mall.

Then, I got a frantic phone call from my son. The dad who'd hired the limo didn't want Cheetah Boy to ride with his son and his date. Apparently, Dad hadn't been warned that his kid had invited classmates to come along. So Dad told my son and another classmate that they had to make other arrangements. Cheetah Boy was close to tears on the phone and announced that he didn't want to go to the prom anymore. Apparently, the other humiliated boy had already left to go home.

"Just come and get me," my son begged. At that moment, my jilted daughter and her friend got into the car.

"Talk to your brother," I told her, handing her the phone. "He doesn't want to go to the prom."

She got an earful while I drove toward the mall, near where I needed to pick up Cheetah Boy as well.

She convinced her brother to go to the prom. He agreed, as long as I would rescue him if he hated it.

Then, he called back and said, never mind, he was going to ride in the limo after all. "But my friend's dad is going to call you. I don't know why," he said.

I dropped my daughter and her friend off at the mall with a wad of cash for dinner. Then, I sat in my car and tried to digest the bewildering events that had just happened.

My phone rang. It was the limo dad. He told me I owed him $50 because he let my son ride to and from the prom in the limo he'd paid for. I told him that I'd be glad to bring the money over right now, because I wanted to tell him in person what a jerk he was. How he ruined the prom for one boy and humiliated my son so badly he didn't even want to go after that.

He blustered for a while, then hung up in my ear. I then texted him to give me his address. He never replied.

Still sitting in the parking lot, it was now around eight thirty at night. It occurred to me that I hadn't eaten all day. I began a mental list of nearby restaurants. And then I got a call from Cheetah Boy.

"Can you come and get me now?" he asked. "I'm over it."

Apparently, his ex-girlfriend, who still came around just often enough to torture him with her unavailability, was all over her new boyfriend, right in front of him. "I'm sitting here all by myself and none of my friends are here," he muttered miserably. I agreed to come and get him, and put the car in gear.

Dinner would have to wait.

A half-hour later, I pulled up in front of the hotel where the dance was being held and phoned my son. "Wait a minute," he told me. A few minutes later, he called back. "The girl I was waiting for just got here, so I don't want to leave anymore," he announced. "I'll find a ride home."

In fact, he ended up going to an after-party and waltzing into the house at four in the morning with a big smile on his face. I guess prom turned out okay for him after all.

Then, I went and picked up Curly Girl and her friend at Starbucks, where they were meeting up with some friends after their elaborate dinner, and their wolf-whistle stroll through the mall.

They ended up having a good night after all, albeit it was not the night they expected earlier in the day. Next year, I'll be urging my daughter to go to prom with her girlfriends. In my era, that wasn't an option, but now lots of kids do it. In that case, I doubt she'll be stood up.

And for the record I finally got to have dinner, even if it was at eleven at night.

## I JUST SENT MY SON AWAY

I DON'T know if you've ever been to Europe, but it's a big, festering cesspool of foreigners, many of whom don't even speak English. (That's a joke, people, don't send me any more hate mail.) Despite this, I just shipped my teenage son there, sending him alone and unprepared into the jungle of the Los Angeles International Airport, otherwise known as LAX, where he boarded transport to another continent.

For the next twenty-two days, he will ride around in a motorcoach with a bunch of other young people, get drunk legally and camp out at night in a tent with strangers. He'll visit countries I've never even seen, all at my expense.

What was I thinking?

Well, if you've ever raised teenagers, you might imagine I thought, "Whew, he's gone for twenty-two whole days."

And that is partly true. It's pleasant to think I could theoretically leave my house overnight and not have to worry it will become Party Zone Number One for every teenager who ever had a Twitter account.

But that's not why I decided to buy him this Contiki young people's tour. That was a reward for his decision to stay in school, when he was considering dropping out of college to get a job.

One day, I was driving him to work when he announced, "Mom, I want to go to Barcelona. I hear the girls are really hot there."

Some of you may know that I have hauled my kids various places in the world, including Africa, Thailand, Egypt, Mexico, Costa Rica, and Italy.

So I enthusiastically said, "Gee, I always wanted to go to Barcelona! So let's go!"

But the look of incredulity on his face told me immediately that a trip to Spain with his mother was not even slightly what he had in mind. Discos that open at midnight were more like it.

I dropped the subject, but I knew about the Australian company Contiki that runs budget tours for eighteen- to thirty-five-year-olds, so I started researching possible trips for him.

I'm not a fan of package tours. You can have more fun and save money traveling on your own, without having to stick to someone else's "If it's Tuesday, this must be Belgium" schedule.

However, Cheetah Boy is too naive to go off on his own. He's not one of those intrepid teens who backpacks around Europe for a year. He can get lost trying to find Disneyland and he's lived in Southern California all his life.

I'd never even let him hold his own passport until I sent him off on Sunday. One of the best things about being a parent is better-late-than-never wish fulfillment. Maybe my parents couldn't afford to buy a trip to Europe when I was his age, but I could send my son, and that was very rewarding to my mother's heart, if not my bank account.

So even though my job prospects seemed shaky at the time, I splurged and bought him an ultra-budget camping trip called the Southern Trail that visited England, France, Italy, Spain, and Greece in twenty-two days, for $2,200, not including airfare, and spent maybe a hundred hours also finding him the cheapest plane flights possible.

"Mom, we're going to see the Eiffel Tower!" my son announced happily, reading the brochure, as I rolled my eyes, thinking of the times I'd offered to take him to Paris. But I was glad he wanted to go.

The trip started in London, and ended up in Athens, Greece. I explained to him that he was going to have to blow up an airbed every night, pitch a tent, and sleep with a strange roomie.

That was okay, he said.

I warned him that he was going to be traveling for days on end on a motorcoach, which he hates, because he tends to get carsick.

That was okay, too.

So I plunked down my credit card, bought him a travel

alarm, new suitcase, and money belt, and dropped him off at the international terminal at LAX on Sunday morning.

He didn't want me to come in with him, because, well, being nineteen, he knows it all. But I'd barely driven out of the airport when he called, because he couldn't find the security gate. Then, he called again, because he still couldn't find it.

By the third call, I told him I was coming back to pick him up, because if he couldn't even get out of LAX, he certainly couldn't find his way around Europe. Miraculously, he then found the gate on his own.

A few minutes later, though, he called. "Mom, I lost my boarding pass."

Just as my heart thudded down to my feet, he announced, "Oh, never mind. I found it."

I was beginning to rue my decision to save a couple of hundred bucks by sending him through Vancouver, requiring him to change planes and then sit through a five-hour layover before boarding a plane to London.

What were the odds he'd actually make it to the United Kingdom? I waited on pins and needles, watching his little icon in the Vancouver airport on "Find My Friends," an iPhone app that allowed me to track his progress wherever he had Wi-Fi.

Then, his little icon disappeared, and I only hoped he had made it onto the plane, while I imagined he'd fallen asleep in the terminal, missed his flight, and would soon be calling me with the bad news.

In the morning, I got word via a friend on Snapchat that he made it to London, found the hotel all by himself after navigating Gatwick Airport, London Victoria Station, and the London Tube, and I let out a huge sigh of relief. Now, he'll be accompanied by a guide and thirty-three other travelers.

He already announced that he planned to find a group

of cute girls and glom onto them, just doing what they tell him. He never has trouble with girls, so I imagine this strategy will work well.

Meanwhile, I'm yearning to know every detail of the trip so far, but I'm not on Snapchat, and we're having trouble communicating except secondhand.

After all, I bought the ticket, the suitcase, the new underwear and socks. As far as I'm concerned, he should wear a GoPro video camera on his head and put the entire trip up on the Periscope app live, so I can watch his travels.

But then, there are those girls. Lots of girls. I probably won't hear from him for a while. I suspect I'll just have to get used to being on my own, too.

## PICTURE THIS: A HAND LIFTING YOUR WALLET

I HEARD some words the other day that struck terror into my very soul: "My son went to get his senior portrait taken."

The reason I was horrified is that "taken" is the operative word here. My friend was about to get taken for a ridiculous amount of money, just because she loves her son.

Senior portraits are only one of the boondoggles that parents of high school seniors face as they propel their children through the last year of free public education. The purchase of grossly overpriced caps and gowns is another, but we'll deal with that later, when it's not an emergency.

Now, it's Red Alert time for senior portrait ridiculousness, which I got sucked into last year, spending $65 on nothing before I managed to pull myself out of the quagmire.

Here's what typically happens: You're just going along, enjoying your summer, when you get a packet in the mail telling you your kid has an appointment on X date to have her senior portrait taken at school. My personal theory is that they do this in the summer, when it's harder for parents to compare notes and realize they're about to be fleeced.

According to this mailer, you need to send your kid along dressed nicely, along with a big fat check. I panicked when I got this mailer from a portrait company last year because my son's appointment was scheduled for the very next day.

So I got him up and sent him off with a check for $65, which seemed excessive to me for school pictures, but what the heck, right? He was a senior and I would have liked to have something to hang on the wall.

Much later, I leafed through the big, fat, glossy brochure that the portrait company sent and realized, oh, crud. I wasn't buying pictures for that $65, I was actually buying nothing except the right to have my kid's picture in the yearbook.

At our school, students are required to sit for these senior portraits or they can't be in the annual. Later, we got some proofs in the mail of attractive shots the company had taken of my handsome boy. The proofs were purposely unusable, having watermarks all over them. Instead, the company wanted me to pay $379 all the way up to $499 for a photo package highlighting the unique charms of my precious one.

Sorry. My precious one doesn't have that many charms, especially when he first wakes up.

I called and told them I'd made a mistake by foolishly thinking I was buying an actual picture I could hang on the wall, so could they please send my $65 back.

You're laughing right now, aren't you? Yeah, that's kind of the reaction I got from them, though they were only laughing on the inside.

Still, I was told that I had paid a $25 "proof deposit," and I could get that much back if I sent back the proofs. The rest of the money went to a "sitting fee" that was shared with the school.

Well, I had no address to mail back the proofs and, soon, my son misplaced them, so I never got my money back.

After I wrote about this in the newspaper, scores of readers wrote to me about their own experiences. Apparently this is a universal boondoggle, though the companies change from school to school. People are fighting mad about it, too, and questioning in particular whether it's fair to leave kids out of the yearbook just because their parents can't afford the sitting fees. Still, most people are unaware of how it works and just go along with the program.

Jack Tingley, who's a retired yearbook sales representative, wrote to me that it's "important that one company take all senior portraits creating matching photos. . . . Using a photo from another photographer would make the yearbook pages look like they have mistaken photos in them."

Stormy Jackson, who graduated from Cypress High School, told me she got more than fifty students to sign a petition asking for a change because they were required to buy a $150 package in order for their pictures to be in the yearbook.

"Not everybody can afford $150, especially with everything else you have to buy as a senior," she said.

Jackson said she was given a fee waiver last year, after multiple requests, and for this coming year, the school is now requiring only a $50 package, and students who ask also can have their fees waived.

Readers in the know recommend going to a Sears or JC Penney portrait studio instead, where they also have caps, gowns, and other props available.

I was lucky that my friend who's a professional photographer ended up taking Cheetah Boy's photos as his graduation present. And they're beautiful. (Thanks, Ana!)

And, listen. If you already did the official senior portrait thing, keep this in mind. I got emails from that portrait company for months after my son's sitting, inviting me to buy the overpriced portraits. And, guess what? The price kept dropping. And dropping.

So keep that in mind if you're tempted. You don't have to buy now. And don't let down your guard, parents. The best is yet to come: The overpriced caps and gowns. The overpriced class rings. And more.

My son was outraged when I immediately threw in the trash the letter he got about the $400 class rings.

"How long would it take you to lose that class ring? Nine seconds?" I challenged him. Not to mention that readers had alerted me that I could have bought a nearly identical ring from Wal-Mart for a quarter of the price.

I did get sucked into buying a letter jacket for my son, who's a jock. I paid $365 at C & L Jackets in Cypress, which was the most affordable place I could find. I got tears in my eyes watching him put it on. He looked so handsome.

It's in the closet. He's never worn it.

## NOT HUNGRY FOR BATTLES AT DINNERTIME

FOR REASONS I can't explain, I continue to engage in the masochistic exercise of "making dinner" every night, even though no one seems much interested except me and the dog.

"Don't eat that—I'm making dinner," I'll tell my teenagers as I watch them haul an Everest-size armload of snacks out of the cupboards.

They look at me as if I'm speaking Vulcan, then walk off, still clutching all the snacks to their chests like a prize.

Why, you're probably asking yourselves, don't I just ban all snacks, period? Well, both my kids were neglected before I adopted them and didn't have enough to eat. I quickly realized that having tons of food in the house they could get any time they wanted made them feel safe.

Now that they're teens, though, it's gotten out of hand.

To keep my blood pressure in check, I've given up arguing with them over eating before dinner. But it invariably means that no one wants my culinary masterpieces when I'm actually finished cooking.

Well, that's not entirely true. Buddy the Wonder Dog never saw a meal he didn't want. Yet another reason to have a dog instead of a child.

When the food is ready, I call my teenage girl child in to eat. She will sometimes actually consume what I've cooked, as long as she didn't just go to In-N-Out with her friends, and as long as none of the food is touching any other food on the plate.

Yeah. There's that touching thing. Funny how she never minds the Oreo sprinkles touching the top of the ice cream sundae. But she won't eat my delicious beef stew because the foods touch each other.

When my kids were little, they ate vegetables and salads without complaint. Well, okay, we mostly ate spinach and broccoli because those were their favorites, but they did eat them. Nowadays, they just look at the green vegetable I've prepared as if it were an agricultural specimen under glass at the Natural History Museum.

"Here, have some spinach," I'll say, making moves to ladle it onto the teens' plates next to the main course.

"Naw, I'll eat some later," they invariably reply. "Later" is their code word for "when pigs fly." And even I'm not stupid enough to think my kid is going to eat broccoli for dessert.

Following the parenting-class advice to "pick your

battles" with teenagers, I usually just shrug and point out that they're jeopardizing their health.

But when Curly Girl again said she'd eat her salad "later," I just snapped and shouted, "Put some salad on your plate now. I mean now! Now! Now!"

She looked at me as if I'd just told her she could never use her iPhone again, burst out crying, and bolted from the room. Okay. I guess I didn't handle that one so well.

This is a girl who would like to help people by giving blood, but the Red Cross won't take her because her iron level is a smidgen too low. I keep pointing out that green veggies provide iron, especially spinach. And she keeps insisting that In-N-Out burgers have plenty of iron as well.

I don't know what teenagers do in other parts of the country, but in our neck of the woods, about one-third of teenagers' annual calorie consumption comes from In-N-Out. It's a daily battle. "No, we're not stopping at In-N-Out for dinner," I insist, as we drive past one of three in our 'hood.

The teens persist. They need In-N-Out, they argue. It's healthy. The fries are made right in front of them.

"I don't care if they cure heart disease—we're not eating burgers three times a week," I argue back. "Besides, I already thawed out a nice chicken for dinner."

Even if I did want an In-N-Out burger—which occasionally I do—the lines of cars in the drive-through that stretch from here to New Mexico would be enough to deter me. Have you ever seen that line? Whew.

So we come home, and the teens grab enough snacks to keep them from starving to death for an hour, until dinner is ready. Then, they'll declare that they really aren't that hungry after all. And I'll settle down for a nice, home-cooked meal, accompanied by the dog.

Luckily, he doesn't mind if his food is touching.

# NO STOPPING THE FRESH INK

NOTHING divides the generations more these days than visible tattoos, which literally illustrate in ink how far apart my views are from those of my teenage children.

I don't know when it became so chic to have needles stuck into your skin thousands of times in the name of art. I'm pretty sure if it were done involuntarily to prisoners, there'd be a huge outcry against it. Petitions would be launched to "Stop the torture!," calling it cruel and unusual punishment.

But these days, young people think nothing of paying big money to have it done to themselves. My twenty-five-year-old friend Alyssa estimates that she's spent $3,000 on tattoos. Admittedly, they're gorgeous but, gulp, very, very permanent. It's even more painful and difficult to have them removed.

Apparently I'm creaky and ancient, because I still think it's peculiar to want to mark up your body with ink that will never come off but will look progressively worse and worse as the years wear on. I don't even like to get ink stains on my fingers, and those wash off with soap.

For what seemed like an eternity, Cheetah Boy threatened to come home with a tattoo. But he held off after I threatened him with imminent death. I also warned him at least 1.2 million times to make sure that any tattoo he got later in life (like, after I passed away) wasn't in a location that would be visible at his job.

You know what's coming next, right?

When he turned eighteen, he began using expressions like, "I'm eighteen, Mom. I got it." I was initially pleased to see he hadn't followed through on his threats to tattoo up.

In June, a friend sent him a $100 bill for a high school graduation present, and I advised him to put it in the bank.

"No, I have plans for this money," he replied.

I was working at home a few days later, when he came in and loitered around my cubbyhole, also known as a corner of our dining room.

"What was the date our adoption was final?" he asked.

"I don't know," I told him, waving my hand. "I'm writing a column. Go away."

"How could you not know when our adoption was?" he said peevishly and stared at me.

I was crabby at this point, but I could see he wasn't going away, so I went to the filing cabinet, pulled out a file, looked it up and told him.

"June 18, 2003. Why do you want to know?" I asked.

He didn't answer, disappeared, and I went back to work without thinking any more about it.

Life went on as usual for a couple of days, until one afternoon, when I looked at his arm and did a double-take. There, still looking red and angry, splayed across the entire inside of his forearm, was a tattoo of my first name and the date of our adoption.

Needless to say, I was greatly touched by this gesture. As one friend said, "He figured out a way to get a tattoo without his mom being mad at him."

I get a little teary-eyed thinking about it. Especially since we hadn't been getting along all that great lately. But I was still irked that he'd placed it on his forearm, where it was visible at his job—all my 1.2 million warnings having been ignored.

Now, he has to wear long sleeves at his restaurant job—where tattoos are banned—or wear the concealing football sleeve that I bought him and he lost in nine seconds. He won't admit it, but I'm thinking he's a little sorry he didn't get it on his shoulder instead.

Many years ago, I interviewed a renowned tattoo artist

who told me he had a few rules: He never tattooed anyone who was drunk or high; and he refused to tattoo anyone's face or neck. He also advised women against tats on their cleavage.

"Someday, honey, you're going to want to wear a fancy dress to a party, and you're not going to want that tat out there," he said he would tell them.

I'm not sure that matters anymore, because tats don't have the stigma they once did.

When I was a child, my black-sheep aunt had an anchor tattooed on her ankle. After she finally sobered up for good, she was deeply ashamed of it, but couldn't afford to have it removed, so she always wore a Band-Aid over it when she was in a dress and stockings.

Nowadays, she probably wouldn't be wearing stockings, and she'd put on an ankle bracelet to make sure everyone saw her tat.

But here's my question: What happens to all that skin when it gets old and saggy?

Yes, kids, it's going to happen. It's slightly terrifying to think of how all that body art could collapse into itself, creating new pictures that no one wants to see nowhere, no how.

And one thing you learn when you get older: Fashions change. It's one thing to have six earring holes in your ear. Take them out and the holes will grow back together. Those huge holes left by plugs are more problematic: You need surgery to fix them.

But imagine when clear, unadorned skin once again becomes hip, probably about the time this generation starts having children. People will be all tatted up and looking like relics from the Jurassic era. (That was an era, right? I know it was a park.) It'll be as revealing about your age as being named Elmer or Mildred, like my great aunt and uncle. Saggy skin, fading ink, and out of fashion. It will be worse than having granite countertops and avocado appliances.

I may have to invest in the laser-removal industry. I have a feeling it will be experiencing a big boom in business.

## PLOTTING REVENGE ON MY TEENS

I'VE BEEN wandering around the Department of Maddening Teenagers.

When my kids were younger, I never even realized this agency existed. But now I can't seem to find my way out. See, here's my problem: I'm trying to figure out a way to survive these seemingly endless years of "almost adulthood" without having an aneurysm burst.

Even though I joke about tequila, I don't really like to drink that much anymore. Becoming slurred and stupid happens naturally these days—adding liquor just makes it worse. Smoking pot makes me paranoid. I'm afraid of prescription pills. I also fear being laughed at if I dared to cart my greatly oversized self into a yoga class. I don't think they make yoga mats in XL sizes.

So what's an overwrought mother to do? I've considered homicide, but they arrest you for that, according to the countless *CSI* spinoffs currently running on TV.

Remember that line Lily Tomlin utters in the movie *9 to 5*? "I'm no fool, I've killed the boss! Do you think they're not gonna fire me for a thing like that?"

Same applies to teenagers, I think. Also, if any more people tell me they understand how difficult the teenage years can be because their straight-A students are now getting B's, I can't be responsible if I run over them with my car.

I recently saw a TV show where a character was deeply upset because her son didn't get into Stanford. Are you freakin' kidding me? I went and sat in a room last week where people were talking about their children's heroin addictions. Get some perspective, Mom. Please.

I'm happy to say that neither of my children is addicted to heroin, but things are still tough at our house right now. I wish I could break my own self-imposed rules and tell you everything. But long ago, I made a vow that I'd never write anything about my kids in this column that would hurt them when the opposition dug it up when they ran for president.

To tell the truth, the odds of either Cheetah Boy or Curly Girl running for president are starting to seem fairly remote, but I still only write about typical youthful foibles, to protect their privacy.

Sadly, serious things happen, too. I would love to write about them, because I know from experience that the parents involved feel sad and alone. And like somehow they're to blame.

Meanwhile, I'm keeping a list of all the ways my teens drive me bonkers, and someday, I plan to wreak revenge by moving in with them.

I will break all their stuff and start shouting when I don't get what I want. I'll tell them "I'll do it later" every time they ask me to get my walker out of the entryway or to pick up my surgical stockings from the living room floor. Then I'll demand they drive me everywhere, change their preset radio stations as soon as I get in the car, steal their phone chargers and then disappear in the mall.

Then, I'll pretend to have sudden mood swings, and go from being lovey-dovey to snapping at them and saying, "You can't make me do that!"

A reader once wrote to me that, now that her sons are adults and living with her again, she sneaks into their trucks at night and changes the radio to country stations they hate.

You go, Mom.

Looking forward to moments like that is all I have right now. Lord help me. I keep playing Gloria Gaynor. "I Will Survive."

## NO, KIDS, LED ZEPPELIN IS NOT A MINERAL

MEMO to my teenagers:

Once upon a time, before you were born, there was a hugely popular and very hairy rock band called Led Zeppelin. Lately, you've been asking me about them, because you've seen news stories about a lawsuit over their most iconic song, "Stairway to Heaven."

Yes, you've heard that song playing in elevators, grocery stores, and pretty much everywhere you go. Yes, they still make gobs and gobs of money every time you do.

I never taught you about Led Zeppelin because I was too busy making you food, hauling you to youth groups and Boy Scouts, and having bitter arguments over homework, But apparently, I am now a Bad Mother because you can't sing "The Lemon Song."

This is according to the fans on my Facebook page, who unanimously voted me Worst Mother of This or Any Other Galaxy for never teaching you anything about Led Zeppelin.

Well, this is what you need to know: When I was your age, we only had one musical device in our house, a big wooden console stereo that occupied ninety percent of the space in our tiny living room.

Hard to believe, right? No, you couldn't stream anything off your mobile devices because they hadn't been invented yet. You had to physically go to a store and shove other teenagers out of the way to get the most popular music when it was put out on the shelves.

If I wanted to listen to a record album (definition: big round black thing that melts when you leave it in a sunny window seat, trust me on that one), I had to go into the living room and play it in front of my stay-at-home mom, who was usually vacuuming our tile floors.

She vacuumed twelve hours a day as a hobby. Usually, she paid no attention to the music I played while she was doing this. The songs could have threatened the imminent destruction of the United States or the rise of Satan's reign, and she would have been oblivious.

But when I proudly pulled out the *Led Zeppelin II* album I'd fought off a pack of other teenagers to buy and put it onto the turntable (a thing that goes around in a circle and plays the aforementioned records), her head popped up from over the vacuum roar.

"WHAT did he just say?" my mom demanded. "What? Squeeze me until the juice runs down my legs?" Her entire face became suffused with red and she glared at me accusingly. "What does THAT mean?"

"Um, I think he's cooking something, Mom," I stammered. "I don't know. I don't really listen to the words."

The song really continues, "The way you squeeze my lemon, I'm gonna fall right out of bed," but I didn't share that with her. Instead, I hurriedly took the record off the stereo and resolved to wait until she was out of the house to play it.

Nowadays, those lyrics actually seem tame compared to some of the hip-hop songs you kids listen to on your iPhones, which seem to revolve largely around becoming intoxicated in clubs and doing unmentionable things to women with ample rear ends.

Since you teenagers control the car sound system (which makes me a wimp but it's better than arguing constantly), I have to click it off about once every nine minutes when something shockingly vulgar comes on.

"Mom, you don't have to turn it off, you could just change the song," you tell me every time.

"No, I actually just want to turn it off," I reply. "I'm not listening to that junk." Then, you are forced into the agonizing task of finding a song on the dial that won't make me shudder, the way Led Zeppelin made my mother shudder.

## FLIP-FLOPS NEVER LEAVE MY KIDS COLD

YES, my friends, winter is officially over, and that means I no longer have to battle with my teenagers over whether they are going to wear flip-flops in the snow.

All right, I'm lying. It doesn't actually snow here in beautiful Orange County, but if we went up to ski country right now, I guarantee you, they would be wearing flip-flops, tank tops, and shorts and complaining about how chilly it is.

"Brrr, it's c-c-c-o-old," Curly Girl would say, as gooseflesh appeared on her naked legs, popping out from the incredible shortness of her short shorts. She only owns one pair of long pants that she finds acceptable to wear, and they have holes deliberately ripped all over them as a fashion statement. It wouldn't matter if we were cruising the coast of Antarctica with a ship filled with legally blind seniors, she would never deign to don any of her seventy-two other pairs of long pants, because they aren't skinny jeans.

Meanwhile, her older brother would be rubbing the muscular arms protruding from his tank top and shivering all the way down past his basketball shorts with the cigarette burn in them that he refuses to throw away.

"Gee, maybe you should put some clothes on, because you're almost naked," is my typical retort.

"No, we're not! We're fully dressed! " they shout back.

Here's the thing about Southern California: Many people simply don't grasp the fundamental purpose of clothing, because they've never lived anywhere it actually gets cold.

My kids will hoot and holler when they see photos of people in Jolly Old England, all dressed up in tweed suits. I try to explain to them that it's cold and damp there, and they're wearing them because wool tweed is a very warm fabric.

A definition here is required for some of you: A warm fabric is one that…keeps people warm.

Sometimes I think people who grew up here believe the purpose of clothing is to have something other than your skin to spill the hot coffee on. If I asked my teens, they'd probably say that clothing exists to:

1. Keep you from being arrested for being naked in public.
2. Provide a fashion statement that identifies you as an intrinsically cool person.
3. Hide unflattering flaws such as hairy backs or bony ribs.
4. Keep the dog's claws from scratching you when he jumps on your lap.

You note that nowhere in the above is the idea that clothing could have been invented to keep a person warm.

After I read *Parenting with Love and Logic*, I stopped nagging my kids every nine seconds about wearing a jacket or even flip-flops in the rain.

It was pointless, because they never listened to me anyway, and then I'd just have an aneurism pop when I looked outside and saw the jacket I insisted they wear hanging on the bushes, abandoned and lonely. I never actually wanted them to freeze to death for failing to take my advice, but it wouldn't hurt them to get a little chilled and wish they'd listened.

As I write this, Curly Girl is up north of Seattle visiting

her birth family. Since rain was forecast, I tried fruitlessly to get her to take some gloves, a hat, and a coat. Instead, she got on the plane with flip-flops and a hoodie. She's texted me a few times, so I guess she hasn't died yet of pneumonia.

And, when I pick her up at the airport tomorrow, I can pretty much guess that she'll be wearing flip-flops. We'll see about the shorty shorts.

## 'MOM, THERE'S NOTHING TO EAT!'

I'VE GIVEN up cooking for my teenagers, because it's like making a pot roast for a bowl of goldfish. They don't want it, they don't eat it, and it costs a lot of time and money.

"Mom, there's nothing to eat," my teens complain to me, as they stare gloomily for several hours at a time into our ginormous refrigerator.

Truthfully, I hate to be hungry, so it's always crammed with so much food that you have to open the French doors gingerly, lest some of it falls out onto your feet.

"Well, there's some chicken drumsticks I cooked for you yesterday that you didn't eat, and sliced turkey and Swiss cheese to make sandwiches, and homemade black bean chili, and blueberries, apples, strawberries, cottage cheese, celery, carrots, yogurt, asparagus, almonds, and cashews. There are eggs, and I made a big salad in the green bowl," I tell them. "You're staring right at it."

"No, Mom," they counter, exasperated. "We don't want any of that."

Of course not. What they want are frozen waffles, or Toaster Strudel, or chimichangas or mini-pizzas, pretty much anything over processed that they can put into the microwave and nuke. Preferably with cheese, or a cheese-like substance. Failing that, they're willing to suffer with

Cap'n Crunch or Froot Loops floating in a big bowl of way too much milk.

I'm not sure at what point the task of eating food cooked by mom became as insufferable to them as listening to opera or cleaning up dog poop. It may have been the moment when In-N-Out burgers also became the ultimate foodstuff. But it's insulting, because I'm a darn good cook.

God help them if they ever move to a state where they don't have an In-N-Out franchise; it might be as unthinkable as me trying to live without Trader Joe's.

When they were little, I'm happy to say, they were never picky eaters, so I didn't have to endure the torment of the damned that I've seen some of my friends go through with their kids. "PLEASE, for the love of God, just try one bite! You'll like it!"

Lately, my teens have eschewed eating anything green, yellow or orange, though they will occasionally deign to eat some berries.

When they were little, they loved cooking with me in the kitchen, and I had visions dancing around in my head of a lifetime of wonderful family meals that we all prepared together, like in the Italian pasta commercials. I suppose I should have been more specific, because nowadays cooking for them involves opening the microwave, seldom a joyful family activity.

When I was their age, my mom was a wretched cook, because she found it a boring chore, but we didn't have many options, with few prepared foods available. Dinnertime was "Eat it or starve" time around our house.

I've tried to make meals tastier for my family, but sometimes I feel like it's a losing battle. Curly Girl has made dinner for all of us a few times. Years ago, that could have been scary, as she tended to experiment with things like a sauce made from ketchup, peanut butter, and cheese, but nowadays she's become more conventional.

I'm becoming accustomed to letting my kids drive, and enjoying the passenger seat, except for the moments of blind, screaming terror.

So maybe, as we go forward, I can turn the cooking chores over to the younger generation, and I'll be the one at the fridge shouting, "There's nothing in here to eat!"

## WHEW, THE KIDS ARE DRIVING ME LESS INSANE

IT'S STARTING to seem like I might actually live through my kids' teenage years, though you wouldn't know it if you listened to them talk, which I try to avoid. They will sit in the car while I'm driving and debate how to divide up my possessions in the event of my death.

"I get the car," one of them will insist, and the other will indignantly argue back, "No, I already put dibs on the car a long time ago. You can have the bicycle."

I usually try to ignore this charming discourse, but eventually I feel compelled to interject.

*"I'm sitting right here, you do realize that?"* I snap at them. "And I have no intention of dying any time soon. At least not until I have moved into your house and tortured the heck out of you."

Cheetah Boy will turn and look indignantly at me, though he won't apologize for his behavior.

"Mom, I can have your house after you die, can't I?"

I usually burst out laughing at this point, and I say, "Sure you can, dude," as I contemplate my ridiculously high mortgage and utilities and the faint likelihood that he'll ever have a job that could pay them.

Interesting things are happening with them. They'll

occasionally say something that borders on intelligent thought, using critical thinking skills that suddenly appear out of nowhere. Maybe they've always had these skills but never felt the need to share them with their mother.

After I sent Cheetah Boy to Europe he now knows the flavors of more beers than I do, but I wasn't really sure what else he learned, except that it rains in Paris and the food in Greece is cheap.

Then at breakfast, Curly Girl, asked me, "Mom, who was Marie Antoinette?" causing me to smack my head against the table repeatedly in despair and ask her, "Didn't you already take world history?"

Apparently she did, but even the fact that this particular French queen was guillotined wasn't enough to make her memorable. I started explaining about her when—greatly to my surprise—my son took over, describing his July visit to the palace at Versailles and how she had lived there.

Now, this might not sound amazing to you, but until that moment I wasn't sure my handsome young man could discourse knowledgeably on any subject that didn't involve using Snapchat, the relative merits of games played on XBox, how to catch a football or why I should give him an extra twenty bucks because he's been doing everything I asked.

He might actually be growing up, I thought to myself, and in her own way, Curly Girl is also displaying greater maturity. They're considerably more fun to spend time with than in recent years past, when they were invariably squirrelly, moody, secretive, and skittish.

If you're going through this yourself, I definitely recommend reading Beth J. Harpaz's book, *13 Is the New 18: And Other Things My Children Taught Me—While I Was Having a Nervous Breakdown Being Their Mother.*

You will be comforted to know it's only a phase. Beth promised me this, and verily it has come to pass. I actually enjoy my kids' company these days, more than I have since they were small, and I can see a day coming when they'll annoy me less and less.

What I can't see happening is the day when they'll stop dividing up their inheritance in advance, so I guess I'd better get going on updating that living trust.

I really don't want them getting any money until they're at least forty, so they won't blow it all in one place. But they really should stop fretting over who's going to get the car. It's such a piece of crap that the answer is probably: the junkyard.

5

MANNERS.
GET SOME.

## RUDE PARENTS SPOIL SHOW

IT'S HARD for me to write this, because I have to acknowledge that there are people at our school who are so rude it defies description.

I just attended two of my kids' school concerts. Both nights I sat next to women who answered their phones and talked while the kids were performing. Why bother to come to the concert at all, if you're not going to actually listen painfully to your kid butchering "Jolly Old St. Nicholas"?

Honestly, I almost ripped the phone out of this one woman's hand, after I turned to her and hissed, "Please get off the phone," and she ignored me and kept yammering away.

The concerts only lasted one hour. What could possibly be so urgent it couldn't wait one hour?

If you thought you might get an emergency call, say, because your house was burning down when you left it, or your husband was in open-heart surgery, you could put your phone on vibrate and stand in the back, where you could go outside and talk if necessary, without disturbing anyone else.

Instead, I had to strain to try to hear Curly Girl sing, and Cheetah Boy play his beginner saxophone.

To add insult to injury, I sat in the last row, in front of another mom who was standing and letting her two four-year-olds sit on the floor directly behind me with coloring books, talking loudly the entire time.

So on one side, I had a woman who wouldn't turn off her phone, and behind me, kids who wouldn't shut up while they were coloring.

I never heard a single "Shush, listen to your brother play" come out of Mom's mouth. Or "Shh, people are listening, please be quiet right now." I guess in her world, it was just fine for kids to make as much noise as they want during a concert.

Note to Mom: A four-year-old is capable of coloring quietly for brief periods of time, with her mouth closed, if someone teaches her to do so. If she can't, then she should stay home with Grandma.

In fact, a four-year-old can listen to her brother or sister play and then applaud afterward, if she's not hideously overindulged.

You know, I really wouldn't have minded so much if I'd heard Mom even once try to quiet the kids down. But she didn't care.

As I was leaving, I mentioned politely to the mom that maybe next time her child could be quiet so I could actually hear my son slaughtering the saxophone. Her response was to ignore me, turn to another mom, and comment on the fact that I am fat.

I didn't say anything else, but I thought to myself, "Yes, it's true I'm fat, but you are stupid and rude, and I would rather be fat any day."

Yeah, so glad these parents are at our school. I'm sure their children will grow up to be just as polite as they are.

## RUDE PEOPLE
## NEVER TAKE A HOLIDAY

THE RUDE parents who ruined my kids' school concerts obviously struck a nerve, because I heard from a lot of people who were also bugged by the epidemic of boorish phone behavior.

My favorite story was the reader who said he went to his nephew's school event and had to listen to a guy talking business on the phone. The guy was so obnoxious, even his wife was telling him to shut up. The reader said he went up, took the guy's phone away, and told him he could have it back after the concert. In my mind, this would have been embellished by applause and a standing ovation from the entire crowd.

I also sent this to our school's principal, who told me in reply that he would be doing something about the phone problem next year. Probably making an announcement before the concert, I imagine, telling people to turn their phones off.

If I were running the event, though, we'd have more fun. I would have the school's vice principal patrol the auditorium, just like they do during the middle school assemblies. She could then confiscate any visible phones from parents, as they do when they see kids holding them.

Wouldn't that be fabulous? Then I would make the parents stop by the office and pick up their phones after the show. If they complained, they could sit down and have detention. Their kids would have to come and pick them up.

And, at least when you're texting, you're not making much noise.

Allow me to also note that in my online Extremely Scientific Poll, readers said overwhelmingly that women are ruder on their mobile phones than men.

So what's with that? I've seen plenty of ill-mannered men, actually, though it is true the two people who annoyed me at my concert were both women.

Readers also mentioned the boorish behavior of people who leave before a concert is over. Our school already deals with that rudeness by telling the kids that their grades depend on them staying until the end of the show, instead of splitting when their part is over.

I say "Yeah" to that. The shows are only an hour long. There's still plenty of time to get home and watch *The Real Housewives of Orange County.*

# YOUR PUBLIC CELL CONVERSATION IS MINE, BUSTER

PLEASE, please keep talking on your cell phone. Do not let my presence disturb you in the least! I want to know all the details of how your husband is a bad lover. And why your cat is coughing up hairballs. And how your foot is healing after surgery.

I live for the chance to sit next to you in the waiting room or at the next table in the restaurant.

And I especially like standing behind you in the checkout line at Target, while you talk with phone in one hand and rummage in your purse for your wallet with the other, while the clerk stands patiently waiting for you to cough up $51.95.

It might occur to some of the many people standing in line behind you that your phone call could have waited five minutes, until you got outside.

Or that you could have found your wallet and credit card while you were waiting, instead of making us all stand there, tapping our toes.

But not me. I was in delicious suspense to find out what happened after your sister lost her keys in the parking lot. Did she find them? Did the Auto Club come? Did she have to walk home?

Sadly, you finally found your wallet and paid, after I was engrossed but before I had a chance to hear the end of the story. I would have followed you out of the store to ask, but Curly Girl was already late for her soccer game, and we were just trying to pick up the team snacks.

I love listening to other people's conversations, and it doesn't bother me that I can only hear one end of the phone, because my imagination can supply the missing speech.

When I'm sitting in a doctor's waiting room, and someone next to me starts in on a nice long chat, I will move next to her and lean closer, so I can really hear what's going on. Sometimes, I'll even comment on the discussion, if I feel I have something to add.

I'm not making this up. I really do this, and you would be surprised how startled and annoyed people get.

"Really! How rude," they'll say, and glare at me when I make a remark about their call, as if I had just grabbed some private body part or committed another unthinkable faux pas.

I then smile and explain that, if they want to have a private conversation, they need to take it outside.

If they are talking in a public place, especially next to me, then I feel it's appropriate for me to join right in.

I admit I don't know too much about gynecological surgery, but that doesn't mean I don't have an opinion to share. That is the American way, right?

People blabbing on their phones in restaurants are another issue entirely. I don't try to butt in on their conversations, but I do feel terribly sorry for the other people at the table. And, if the talker is alone and turns away, I always just snatch one little taste off her plate. Really, she'll never notice.

So keep talking on your phone. Please. At least until my own food arrives or they call me into the doctor's office.

## EXCUSE ME, GET YOUR TOWEL
## OFF MY LOUNGE CHAIR

SO HERE'S a vexing problem I want you to solve for me: You're vacationing at a resort that is costing you $1.2 trillion a day. You come out to the pool or beach. There are lots of empty lounge chairs, but they seem to have invisible occupants who have left towels on them, carefully draped and folded to convey ownership.

I'm not talking about when people throw their detritus on a chair, as sunscreen, flip-flops, and such, and then dive into the pool or walk over to the bar to get a margarita. You know what I mean. The glaring striped towel that says, "I was here first, but now I've gone back to bed so keep your greedy little mitts off this lounger because I might come back someday. Or maybe I won't."

What exactly is the etiquette in this situation? Where's Emily Post when I need her?

Listen, I'm not slamming people for reserving beach chairs; heck, I've done it myself. Staying at a resort in Cancun, I realized the very first morning that if I didn't get up at sunrise, hustle down to the pool in my pajamas, and slap a towel on a chair, there wouldn't be a lounger available within 100 miles when I actually woke up, ate breakfast, and came downstairs.

This presents a bit of a pickle. One wants to honor the intentions of the fine Early Birds who were so perspicacious as to get up and reserve their spots. It takes a certain amount of gusto to wait for the sun to come up and then pelt down to the beach to stake out your spot.

On the other hand, why should chairs sit empty when others want to use them? Should I be forced to sit on the scorching concrete or the white-hot sands just because you thought—maybe—you might want to use a chair and then changed your mind, forgot all about it, and went into town to buy a pair of wooden tongs?

If I remove "your" towel and sit down on "your property," am I going to worry every minute that you might show up and yell at me? Not the relaxing Zen vacation I had envisioned.

Now, this is decidedly a First World problem, no question about that. We're all lucky to be at a resort worrying about deck chairs, instead of, well, you can think of the alternatives.

But this was on my mind lately, because a friend and I bought day passes to a fancy hotel pool in Newport Beach. We can't afford to actually stay there, you understand. But we can afford to use the pool. Reading the reviews, it seems like we have the towel slapping problem going on there, so I'm wondering if there will be any chairs to sit in when we arrive.

I know that some hotels have a policy of removing towels if the chairs have clearly been unoccupied for half an hour. I wish they would all do this.

One of the readers on my Facebook page also told me that her sister always tips the pool guy to save chairs for them and set out a bucket of ice. Now, I'm not even going to get into the etiquette of doing this except to ask the important question: "Why don't they ever invite me?"

Apparently, this is also an issue on cruise ships, where you're also paying big for what is essentially a very tiny bit of real estate. One reader told me she lay next to four chairs that were empty except for towels. Several sets of people came by, removed the towels, enjoyed the chairs, and then left before the original owners finally showed up, retrieved their belongings, and left without ever even sitting in the chairs.

This hasn't ever happened at my gym (although people do other annoying things like talk on their phones in the sauna), but another reader told me that people "save" showers in her gym's locker room by hanging their towels and shampoo bags outside of them until their workouts are over: "Once I used one of these 'staked-out' showers and the lady opened the shower curtain and screamed at me! I have no idea what she said because it was in another language, but it prompted me to complain about shower saving to the management on my way out."

Yikes. Yet another reason to never go to the gym. Or never take a shower. Your choice.

Right now, some of you might be grinding your teeth and thinking of situations where the "chair saving" also got out of hand. So, what are the rules? When is it okay to save, and when is it just plain rude?

I think most people agree that it's kosher if one person stays to babysit the saved resource, be it a lounge chair or a firepit. Right? At least someone's making an effort to stake a claim. But, hmm, ponder this.

I remember going to my kids' school concerts and having to sit in back because families up front thought nothing of saving ten seats, taking up an entire row for family members who were nowhere in evidence. Why should I have to sit in the back row because your Uncle Harvey is late?

Sometimes it was tempting to make some sort of fake badge, pin it on, and then just go and remove all the stuff off the saved seats. Or tell people, "You can save two seats. That's all. Next time, tell your Aunt Minnie to be on time." Considering how painful I found my kids' musical recitals (just kidding, kids, you were wonderful and I loved every second), maybe Aunt Minnie could just supply the cake afterward.

Meanwhile, I think I'll just adopt the advice of some of my other Facebook fans. They told me to show up at the pool, wait half an hour, and if no one shows up, remove the towel, fold it up, and put it under the chair. Then, sit down. If the erstwhile owner shows up, just say sweetly, "Oh, sorry. There wasn't any towel on this chair. The pool staff must have removed it." Ooh, did I really say that? Gee, I would never, ever tell a lie. Guess there really wasn't a towel. Wink, wink.

# I LOVE NOT HEARING YOU BRAG ABOUT YOUR KID

IT'S AWARDS season for schools as they close up shop for the summer. And you know what that means. Everyone will be boasting about their kids' fabulous achievements: The trophies. The medals. The certificates. The prestigious universities that are fighting over the chance to have their kids grace their halls.

"Here's a photo of Johnny Jr. as he's the youngest boy ever elected to Congress," your slight acquaintance will press upon you, pulling out her phone. "Oh, and here he is giving a sold-out bassoon recital at Carnegie Hall."

Her smartphone's photo album is full of proof that her gene pool is better than yours, and she wants to share it all with you after she's trapped you at the grocery store or as you try in vain to get a doughnut after church.

"Oh, and here's little Sarah, heading off to the U.S. Olympic Training Center for the summer," she squeals. "You heard she made the team, right?"

Meanwhile, you're sitting there thinking, "I'm just glad my kid graduated—by the skin of his bleeping teeth. He's alive. He has all his teeth and limbs. He's not shooting heroin. So we're good."

I've written before about parent envy, and a lot of you responded. No matter how egregiously people brag about their kids and how obnoxious it is, you're not allowed by rules of proper etiquette to tell them to shut up. You're not allowed to use an air horn or pepper spray them, either. Or a Taser. I found that out the hard way. Sad, really.

People wrote to me and said, "My child is autistic, and I consider it an achievement when he ties his shoe, so, yeah, I don't need to hear about your brilliant progeny."

Another woman wrote that her son had died tragically, so it's not just annoying but actively painful to have other people's children's accomplishments shoved in her face.

This is irritating enough after church, and an excuse for murder when you see someone else grab that last chocolate doughnut before you can reach it. But now, due to the marvels of modern technology, you can be harangued twenty-four hours a day, seven days a week. All you have to do is log on to Facebook.

Honestly, when I glance at Facebook and see that someone I barely know has just posted photos of her kid's acceptance letters to elite schools, it just makes me want to punch my fist through the wall.

"Which one of these fabulous schools should my kid attend?" the post continues.

Yeah, that's one of the burning issues of our time. Thanks for asking me to ponder it for you, even though you're almost a stranger.

My kid might make it to college someday, after she gets out of rehab.

(I'm just kidding. Curly Girl is not in rehab. I was trying to make a point.)

Did it occur to you that it's nice to celebrate your achievements, but maybe not brag about them to everyone you ever met?

And, yes, I say "your" achievements, because obviously you are posting this because you take tremendous pride at having encouraged, driven or hounded your offspring to this place in life.

Just so you know for the future, you can change your Facebook settings so that only "close friends" can see those letters. That way, only your BFFs and your family can rejoice with you about Junior's accomplishments.

And the rest of us can go on with our petty, mundane, non-award-winning lives in peace. And maybe get that last doughnut. I know, I know. I really don't need it.

6

# HOUSEKEEPING

## MY HOUSEKEEPER
## IS WORTH MORE TO ME THAN GOLD

MY FAVORITE day rolls around every two weeks, and I'm not talking about payday (though that's up there pretty high as well). That is the day my housekeeper comes to rescue me from my own sloth, and I never get tired of it, or bored by repetition, even though it occurs every two weeks. (I'm calling her Ronda, but that's not her real name.)

Author Erma Bombeck once said that cleaning your house while the kids were still growing is like sweeping your porch while it's still snowing, and I think that's true, but I still look forward to it.

Here are the happy stages of "Ronda the Housekeeper Day":

### Stage One

Go to the ATM and get some cash, because my kids always suck up any excess I have lying around. I pay Ronda around $20 an hour, which I think is fair for five hours of manual labor cleaning my toilet and mopping my floors. Occasionally, someone will act surprised at this, and insist they can get me someone cheaper.

"Gee, I know someone who will clean your whole house for $30!"

Well, here's the thing: I'm not interested in exploiting people just because they're desperate and will work for less. Ronda came to this country from Guatemala (she's in this country legally now, so don't send me any hate mail, thank you) as a mom deserted by her abusive, alcoholic husband. She left her boys with her mother and came up here to find a job to support them. At first, she told me, she worked for room and board only, which in my mind sounds an awful lot like slavery. Not the only time I've heard that kind of story, by the way. I pay her what I think is fair, and if you bargain your cleaning lady down to get her to scrub your floors for less, I probably wouldn't like you.

## Stage Two

Scurry around and put away anything that I think might get misplaced. Two women putting things away in the same kitchen is never a good thing. I spend a lot of time pacing and thinking, "Dang, where would she have put the measuring cups?" It's just easier to put them away before she gets here. I usually throw a load of towels in the washer to give her a head start, since she does our linens. Sometimes I'll wipe up the dog vomit or something else that's particularly disgusting, though I'm not one of those people who cleans the house before the housekeeper arrives. I've always been a little confused by that concept. I know there are a lot of you out there, so please explain it to me.

## Stage Three

Greet Ronda when she arrives, then vamoose as quickly as possible.

I don't want to be around while she's cleaning for two reasons. First, because I can tell I'm getting in her way, though she would never say so. The second and more important reason is that I feel guilty. I feel vaguely ashamed that I'm making someone else clean the gunk out of my bathroom sink, even though I know she wants and needs the work.

Best-selling author Barbara Ehrenreich wrote a piece for Harper's magazine back in 2000 called "Maid to Order: The Politics of Other Women's Work" that I could never get completely out of my head. She went to work as an employee of one of those corporate housekeeping companies for the experience, so she could write about it from an informed perspective.

She wrote that people like to hire cleaning services because they needn't have a relationship with one person and watch her scrub their bathtub. Seriously, do you really think those maids are merry? Because I'm pretty sure they're not.

Some people also worry about theft, though I've never had a problem. One of my former housekeepers, who fled the death squads in El Salvador, had been a college professor there, and the only problem I had with her was letting her finish her work, because she was so interesting I always just wanted to talk. My mother was a neat freak who grew up an orphan in Texas, where, in those days, the difference between "white trash" and respectable folk was how clean they kept their houses. My mom could never abide the fact that her daughter was clearly trash.

### Stage Four
Come home to a sparkling, lemon-scented house with freshly folded towels and clean sheets, enjoying an hour of pure bliss after walking through the door. At this point, I might think about how I really can't afford a housekeeper and wonder which kid I should get rid of so I can continue to hire her services.

### Stage Five
It's been twenty-four hours since Ronda was here, and I'm wondering how my house could possibly look so trashed. I also wonder why my son needs five towels for one shower, and why he can't pick them up off the floor. There's nothing to be done but pine for her next visit. Ronda, please come back!

## SERIOUSLY, CAN IT BE THAT HARD
## TO PUT AWAY A SPOON?

IF I WANTED to learn to play spoons, I'd really be in trouble. Because it's impossible to find a spoon in my house, even for a prosaic task like stirring my coffee.

When Cheetah Boy and Curly Girl moved in, it never occurred to me that I would never again be able to open the silverware drawer without a momentary shiver of fear and dread. Will there be a spoon in the drawer to taste the soup? Will there be a fork to stick in the broccoli steaming on the stove?

This has become a mystery and a crapshoot, like betting on the horses every single day.

While this has its thrilling moments, it does get tiresome, especially when I'm reduced to trying to spread peanut butter on bread with a fork while making school lunches in the morning in a coffee-deprived condition.

I grow tired of opening up the dishwasher and hoping against hope that I will hit the jackpot there, only to have my dreams dashed once again.

The problem is twofold. There's the lack of a useful implement to perform a simple household task, like checking to see if the spaghetti sauce needs more salt. But the even larger problem is the extreme spike in my blood pressure when I think of the 1,270 spoons and forks I have put in that drawer since 2003, and the headache it gives me wondering where they all have gone.

I have taken action to avoid this headache, including the following steps:

- Joining a "Moms With Missing Cutlery" support group.
- Locking the kids in their rooms until they locate five items buried beneath the rubble.

- Checking the flower beds for spoons used as digging implements.
- Installing a metal detector over the top of the garbage can.
- Having a ghost hunter come and banish any poltergeists.
- Buying ninety-two new pieces of silverware at a thrift shop sale.
- Putting pictures of the missing items on the back of milk cartons.

All these things gave me the foolish confidence that when I opened the silverware drawer, I would find something there. But of course, they were all in vain. Putting more spoons in the drawer only meant there were more to lose.

Considering I'm constantly pestering my kids to use their utensils when we sit down to meals, and stop acting like they were raised by wolves, you'd think there would be more of them around. I mean, what are they using them for? Not for eating, that's for darn sure.

I recently went on a hunt through my house, and (this is true) I found spoons in the following locations:

- Stuck under the kitchen cabinets.
- On the kids' bathroom counter.
- On the kids' bathroom floor.
- Behind the kitchen garbage pail.
- On Cheetah Boy's dresser, next to the week-old bowl of cereal and milk.
- On Cheetah Boy's desk, next to the empty bottle of Gatorade.
- On Curly Girl's floor, underneath the pile of clothes.
- Under Buddy the Wonder Dog's water dish.
- And, amazingly enough, one lonely spoon lying all by itself in the drawer.

I really didn't intend to write this column, because it wasn't that long ago I told you about missing scissors, and I thought you'd be over the topic of missing metal. But I got so many letters begging me to write about this crisis that I feel obliged to respond.

And I know, Mom, if I quit my job and stayed home and cleaned fourteen hours a day as you did my entire childhood, things would not go missing for so long.

But I would probably be missing, because they would have carted me away in a straitjacket. Though if my kids keep trying, they might get me there yet.

I might just be one spoonful away.

## LET'S TALK ABOUT WASHING THE DISHES

MANY of you have experienced this chore in your lifetime, but some of you have not.

For example, I would bet all my milk money that my daughter's twenty-one-year-old boyfriend, who lives at home with his family, has never touched a dishrag in his life, even though he's an employed adult who eats food quite regularly. It's going to be a major shock when he finally moves out and discovers that dishes really don't wash themselves. Though if he gets himself the kind of wifey that my daughter will never be, maybe he won't.

My kids have always treated dirty dishes as if they were covered with spent nuclear waste, and they'd have to go into an isolation chamber if they so much as brushed against one of them.

We've had a dishwasher in our kitchen for a long time now, but even that seems potentially deadly to them, apparently, because they pick up the dishes so gingerly and throw them in there with such force that it's a miracle from Lourdes that any of them survive.

I point out that we have rubber gloves, but finding and putting them on involves extra work they're not willing to take on. It's hard even to get them to unload the clean dishes, but I always insist.

See, I remember being a kid, when my sole purpose in life was to make it so aggravating for my mother to force me to do chores that she would simply do them herself. I got out of so much work by driving her crazy, and I refuse to give my adult children the satisfaction.

I'm too mean and cranky to have a husband, but let me just say this about guys: Your work is entirely suspect. Now, I don't mean all you guys. Some of you are quite tidy. In fact, I dated a guy who was so persnickety he used to rearrange all the dishes after I put them in his dishwasher, because they didn't meet with his exacting standards. I couldn't marry him, though. I would never have measured up.

I used to be one among a group of friends who went camping together every Memorial Day, before we got lazy and booked cabins instead. I remember one night when we ladies cooked a big dinner, and the guys offered to wash up. None of us was paying any attention to the washing process going on behind us until one of my girlfriends came over, looking like she'd just seen Bigfoot on the way back from the john.

"They're not using any soap," she hissed. "I was just watching the guys wash and they're not using any soap." Yikes. Good job, guys. You managed to get out of washing all dishes, forever.

I do remember when I had my first apartment—back in the days when low rents meant a single gal could actually afford to live alone. I would let the dishes pile up in the sink on the theory that the mold they generated could produce penicillin that would be beneficial to mankind. (That was also the time in my life when I would simply buy new undies because I hated the laundromat.)

When people came over, I'd just put the dirty dishes in the never-used oven. Recently, I read a Dave Barry column where he discussed the practicality of putting them in the freezer instead, where they would retard mold. Too bad I never thought of that.

Over the years, various roommates and I had spats over whose turn it was to wash, or to unload the dishwasher. I do believe dishwashing is the No. 1 cause of arguments among people who live together, according to my Extremely Scientific Survey of my own past.

I know guys—and you possibly do too—who simply use paper plates and disposable cutlery for everything so they don't have to wash. But that just seems like going over the edge. I mean, no one in my family is actually Oscar Madison from *The Odd Couple*.

Apparently, I'm not the only one who finds the topic divisive, because there's a YouTube video out there that's been seen 1.2 million times called "How to Wash a God*#@n Dish."

"If your roommate sent you this video, they're concerned you may not know how to get off your (bleep) and wash a (bleeping) dish for once in your pathetic life. Don't worry, washing even one (bleeping) dish isn't that hard," the narrator tells the viewer. "It's so easy, there's no reason not to do it, you entitled little piece of (bleep.)"

Good thing there wasn't any YouTube back when I had roommates.

**7**

# BAD MOM—
# BAD, BAD

## HOW TO BUG YOUR KIDS TO DEATH

OUR SCHOOL librarian gave my son a copy of the book *101 Ways to Bug Your Parents*, by Lee Wardlaw. It was an old copy, and she told him he could keep it.

This was really annoying for a parent whose children were already naturally talented in this regard. I was tempted to take that book over to the librarian's house and give it to her kids.

This volume has all sorts of fabulous ideas like, "Ask for a big breakfast and then say you're not hungry." Or, "Use all the hot water in the shower." It's not like children need lessons on this stuff. They do just fine with no instruction at all.

But occasionally, when my rugrats have been particularly aggravating, I want to exact my revenge. That's why I have my own list of things I can do, such as:

**Dancing.** My kids go into a frenzy of mortification if they see me shake any part of my body to music. It's even worse, of course, if I dance in public, like at a wedding, but even waltzing around the house sends them into a medical state of shock.

**Singing the wrong words to songs.** Kids absolutely hate it if you make up your own words to songs they know by heart. The other night, we were watching *The Brady Bunch*, and I started singing the Brady song along with the characters, but doing it wrong on purpose. My son was so upset he almost had to go to bed.

**Stop talking suddenly when they come into the room.** They will think you're hiding something and it will simply drive them mad, even if you know all you were really talking about was the hairballs spit up by your cat.

**Putting my arm around them in public.** This is mostly a problem of Cheetah Boy's, but even Curly Girl is starting to act like my arm is a heat-seeking missile if it lands anywhere on her body in public.

**Having your own tantrum.** Sometimes, Cheetah Boy would sit down on the floor and start screaming when he didn't want to do a chore. When I was in the mood, I would sit down next to him, and start screaming, too. This never failed to infuriate him, and amuse me. Sometimes, he would get so mad he would forget what he was yelling about.

**Coloring my hair.** Before I had kids, I was under the mistaken impression that my hair belonged to me. Now, every time I want to change the color even slightly, my children feel it's a personal attack on their emotional stability.

**Going back to bed.** When my kids are arguing with each other or refusing to follow my instructions, sometimes I just get fed up, go into my bedroom, and silently crawl into bed. It feels delicious, by the way, for the brief time I'm allowed to be in there before the kids are on my bed, begging me to get up and promising to behave better.

**Refusing to get off the phone.** My children have no interest in me whatsoever until someone calls, which is their signal to ask me every question they forgot to ask all day long. Occasionally, though, I will simply refuse to answer them, and they will finally give up and let me talk.

Awww, aren't Cheetah Boy and Curly Girl sweet? Well, most of the time. As for the rest, then they're the motivation behind counter-irritation strategies.

## SORRY I'M SO STUPID, BUT WHAT WAS YOUR NAME?

ONE OF the more embarrassing aspects of having children is that you meet so many people whom you know by sight, but you couldn't recall their names on a bet.

My kids played both soccer and baseball. This meant

that every week I was involved with four teams that had kids, parents, and coaches, few of whom I had ever met before.

Some of the parents seemed to have an uncanny ability to remember everyone's names. This only made it more embarrassing that I couldn't recall anyone's except the coaches.

"Hey, err, kid, great game!" I mutter to every player, hoping they don't notice I have no idea what they're called. Meanwhile, parents who are more observant have been cheering my kids on by name since the first day.

This is only made worse by the fact that even when I do know someone's name, I call them by the wrong ones, even Cheetah Boy and Curly Girl.

"How's Justin doing?" I recently asked some parents I like at the ballpark, whose son had been to our house numerous times. "His name is Zachary," his mom retorted.

Oops. Well, someone on that team was named Justin.

I have resorted in fact to calling everyone "Bud" or "Chica" depending on whether they are male or female. It makes me wish everyone could just wear name tags all the time.

Our church actually created permanent name tags for everyone to wear, which was a great idea, except we lost ours in five minutes.

So now, every Sunday morning, we walk around smiling and talking to people I've seen every Sunday for five years, but I have absolutely no idea who they are. I've been in deep, passionate discussions with people whom I now know a great deal about—except what they're called.

After you've talked to someone every week for five years, it's far too late to admit you don't know their names, especially if you have reason to think they know who YOU are.

I have resorted to poring over the pictures in the church directory and trying to memorize names for future reference.

So if I run into you at the park, school or the church, and

I call you Bud or Chica, please don't be offended. I do it to my own kids. And, if you want to tell me your name, I would be grateful. But don't be surprised, if, the next time I see you, I have already forgotten.

## IT'S APPARENT I HAVE NO CLUE

WHEN they passed out the parenting manual for raising kids, I didn't get one. I was too busy talking to my friends in the back of the class.

Oh, wait, that's my son, according to his algebra teacher. But that's another subject.

In any event, it is frequently brought to my attention that I'm doing things all wrong. Sometimes, this information comes from Cheetah Boy and Curly Girl, who are now adolescents and old enough to know how they're supposed to be raised.

"Stop shouting," Cheetah Boy will tell me, when I discover that he's gotten another F on a test. I usually decline to follow this advice, even though I know shouting isn't necessarily the best way to handle this news.

They also advise me to stop cursing, which admittedly I should do, and to "chillax," which is apparently a verb designed to raise my blood pressure even higher than it was before.

Readers also write to give me parenting advice, some of which is excellent, some not so good.

Some readers just tell me to get the heck out of their newspaper, either because they find my attempts at humor annoying, or because I'm just too darn fat.

To those readers who write and tell me to lose weight, because I'm too ugly to be in their paper, I'll make you a deal. I'll lose weight when you stop drinking a case of beer every night, beating your kids and embezzling from your boss.

Fat people don't have more problems than anyone else, they just wear them on the outside, where they make easy targets for people who've gone off their medication.

I had one reader call me to task for daring to call my kids' orthodontia a "cosmetic procedure." You're right, ma'am. Clearly it's right up there with brain surgery as a medical necessity.

One reader named Chris wrote to me after I wrote about my son being embarrassed by me at his Pony League baseball games. In the interest of embarrassing him further, I asked readers to give me suggestions.

Chris said the best way to embarrass a teen at his game is to wear brightly colored shoes and a yellow T-shirt with his team number and the slogan "World Champion" emblazoned on it, while calling his name. Then offer to pose for pictures afterward with his friends.

Other readers had similar suggestions, including wearing a T-shirt with his picture on it and shouting his special nickname out loud.

I took my kids to an Angels baseball game not long ago as a family outing, but Cheetah Boy ran into some friends and went to sit with them instead. This irritated me, so I spent the rest of the game blowing him kisses and telling him in sign language how much I loved him. He didn't care too much for this, but his friends found it amusing.

Recently, I wrote about my difficulty deciding what to do when my kids lie to me. Talk to them? Seek a grand jury indictment?

I got a long, interesting email from a Dr. Catherine Bailey, whom I don't know, but who really sounds like a woman who knows what she's talking about.

She told me that she thinks "most kids are like cats. They want what they want, when they want it and you get their attention by being the provider of the goodies, which of course are provided when they are on track. Not on track, no goodies."

She added that "raising kids is a lot like herding cats. If they are generally moving in the right direction, it's good enough."

Well, thanks, Catherine. I do know rather a lot about herding cats, after spending the past twenty five years around newspaper reporters. So that's some darn good advice.

## I'LL GET EVEN WITH MY KIDS SOMEDAY

RAISING KIDS can be such an indescribable joy that you wonder how anyone could miss this peak experience. And it can plunge you into the depths of despair.

I've been known to feel both emotions within the same hour.

When I'm in the pits and my kids are driving me bonkers, I like to plot my revenge. This gives me something to do while I'm sitting in the orthodontist's office reading an old copy of *People*, at the freezing cold ballgame wrapped in a blanket, or sweltering at the pool, waiting for the kids to reappear.

I just try to remember that eventually, preferably later rather than sooner, I'll be a little old lady who needs a lot of care. I plan to move into my kids' house, where they might get a little payback.

Here are things I plan to do when that day comes:

- Complain that it's not my turn to clean up the kitchen, because I did it yesterday.
- Take all the towels out of the bathroom and throw them on my bedroom floor. Then walk on them.

- Ask for cash every day and when asked what I spent yesterday's cash on, glare at the speaker and say, "I dunno."
- Suddenly refuse to eat food that I formerly loved, especially when I know it was purchased in bulk.
- Remove the switchplate covers from the light switches on the wall for no apparent reason and throw them away.
- Toss my clean clothes into the dirty clothes hamper, because I'm too lazy to fold them and put them away.
- Whine that "All the other moms get to do it!"
- Walk into the living room at 8:40 at night and announce that I have a big project due the next day and need to go to the store for supplies.
- No matter what they make for dinner, say I'm not hungry, then thirty minutes later demolish the kitchen making a messy snack, making sure to leave all the food wrappers open and on the counter.
- Eat in my room and hide my dirty dishes under the bed, even if there is food on them.
- Hide all the scissors in the house so no one can find them.
- Throw one spoon a day in the trash instead of the sink.

## GAINING A CLUE
## IS MY FOOTBALL FIELD GOAL

AT AGE fifty-five, I was starting to think I'd make it through the rest of my life without having to do certain things: bungee jumping, going to federal prison, watching Maury Povich, or sitting through another football game.

I never learned the rules of football and could not care less.

Decades ago, back when fish were climbing onto dry land, I did time in my ugly green pep club uniform, cheering on my high school team, utterly ignorant of most anything happening on the field.

I hoped then to live the rest of my life pigskin-free.

But that was before my fourteen-year-old Cheetah Boy began playing freshman football.

Now, I do time in the stands every week, gnawing on my knuckles, worried that those other boys might knock him over, get him dirty, or, egads, even break a fingernail.

It's my bad luck that he's one of his team's best players, meaning that sometimes they give him the ball. Even I have not failed to notice that players with the ball frequently get knocked down. This is not a good thing, my maternal instincts say.

It's beginning to dawn on me that I may actually have to learn something about the game, because I seem like an idiot sitting up there, pathetically imploring the other parents to explain to me what is going on.

I bought the book *Football for Dummies*. Seriously. I really did.

And it helped, but not entirely. There are still some questions that have been puzzling me at every game.

1. Why are those guys on the field wearing striped shirts? (a) Stripes were very big at New York Fashion Week this year. (b) There was a really good sale at Macy's.

2. Why do those guys throw their yellow hankies up in the air? (a) They are trying to determine the direction of the wind. (b) They are expressing a breach of etiquette.

3. What are those guys in striped shirts doing when they wave their arms on the field? (a) The YMCA dance (b) The Macarena

5. Why does that player stick his hands underneath the other player's rear end? (a) To warm them up. It's cold on the

field. (b) He likes him. He really, really likes him.

6. Why does the winning team dump Gatorade on the coach? (a) Because he is starting to smell (b) It would go bad if it sat in the locker room for a week.

7. Why is the coach making strange hand signals from the bench? (a) He wants to make an obscene gesture at the guy in the striped shirt, but parents are watching. (b) He's telling his wife to start the car so he can make a quick getaway.

8. Why aren't there any girls out there playing football? (a) Girls have more sense. (b) The pads would make them look fat. (c) Helmets would smash their hairdos. (d) All of the above.

## I MISSED THE MEMO ON THE FATE OF PANTYHOSE

OCCASIONALLY, I think I might be a better mother if I could get inside my teenagers' heads and think as they do. Of course, this is also a scary idea, especially after you've seen a certain number of movies based on scientific experiments that have gone wrong.

"The woman who got trapped inside her kid's head!" the trailer would boom as I rolled around in there bouncing from a pile of dirty clothing to an amorphous pit filled with obscene hip-hop lyrics.

I can only imagine feeling the hot flashes accompanying jolts of hormones and the extreme mortification involved in seeing or doing, well, nearly everything.

A small part of me thinks it would be nice to be a teenager again, with my whole life stretched out before me. But then I realize that I'd have to give up so many things, such as the memory of what pioneering life was like before iPhones, personal computers, microwave ovens, and even pantyhose.

You men won't relate in the slightest, which is perhaps the reason pantyhose never made a list of top inventions of the twentieth century. But believe me, to women, they seemed virtually miraculous at the time—no more garter belts! Especially considering that, in those days, some of us were wearing mini-skirts so short that we couldn't even pick up a dropped pencil without flashing the entire universe.

More than once, I remember dropping something, looking down at it, considering it, then just walking on by. I didn't need it that badly.

Hard to imagine, but pantyhose are now becoming obsolete. Of course, they always were this very strange accessory—that you knew could be ruined instantly by a fingernail.

I didn't even know they'd gone out of fashion until I demanded that my Curly Girl wear pantyhose with her silvery sandals under her prom dress. I made a special trip to the store to buy them.

"What are these things?" she demanded, making a sour lemon face as she took them out of the wrapper. You would have thought I was trying to cram her into a corset or a bustle.

"They're stockings," I said, apparently providing her with a lesson in ancient history. "You need to wear them under your dress."

"Why?" she demanded. "I'm not wearing those things." And she stomped off to sulk.

I became incensed and looked for comfort, as I often do, from other mothers on my Frumpy Mom Facebook page, who certainly would understand the gaucherie of being bare-legged beneath a formal dress.

I was disappointed.

"No one wears pantyhose anymore," was the general consensus. "How is she going to show off her mani-pedi?"

What? When did that happen? I thought I was a hip and groovy mom who was on top of the latest trends. I took my kids to see Eminem and Rihanna at the Rose Bowl, for pete's sake.

How did I miss the memo on pantyhose? I don't know if this is only a California thing or not. I suspect that in ZIP codes where it actually gets cold in the winter, stockings might not be so declasse.

I used to wear not one but two pairs under my dresses when I stood out shivering in the snow, waiting for the school bus in Clinton, Utah.

But in those days, I'd really never even heard of a pedicure, nor did I know anyone who'd ever had one. And people weren't wearing too many strappy sandals in the winter.

Oh, allow me to digress for one minute and tell you that I just got the first mani-pedi of my life. My daughter insisted we get one while we were on vacation in Sonoma County.

I'd always resisted, partly because I'm the daughter of a cattle rancher who thought such things were ridiculous. Also because I couldn't imagine having some poor soul cleaning my feet, unless it was a religious ritual in church. Oh, and I'm terribly ticklish.

Let's just say that I did it for my daughter, and I liked it. It probably won't be fifty-nine years until I do it again. I satisfied my dilemma over someone working on my feet by leaving a huge tip. The ticklish part—well, let's just say I made everyone in the salon laugh. But then, that's my job.

So could I get into the head of a person who thinks mani-pedis are a human need like eating? And who can't conceive of life before text messages?

Well, maybe not. So I'll just keep my brain intact. Because, maybe someday I'll once again need to know how to operate a fax machine.

# WAS I TAUGHT HOW TO TALK TO MY KIDS BY WOLVES? APPARENTLY

A WHILE back, I hauled my teenagers off to family therapy so we could all learn to get along better without entertaining the neighborhood with our spats.

Yes, it's true. We never got dramatic enough to make it onto *The Jerry Springer Show*, but we did occasionally provide viewing for the entire neighborhood, as we aired our family disputes loudly on the front lawn.

Some of you write to me and say things like, "You're such a good mom," and I think to myself, "That's so nice, and so completely untrue."

Anyway, this therapist gave me a list of things I was never supposed to say to my teenagers, and I read it out loud. Then, I read it again, and again with my mouth agape, because I couldn't believe what I was seeing.

There was nothing on that list that I didn't say to my kids all the time. In fact, that pretty much summed up most of our conversations.

Admittedly, I already knew I shouldn't snap at my kid that he was a lazy oaf when he ignored my third command to take out the trash. Though, sometimes I still did.

But even the things that I thought were positive, it turned out I wasn't supposed to say. Such as, "You're so smart, I know you could be doing better in school if you try."

Or, "Don't get stressed out, it's only high school. It's not worth worrying about."

Apparently, those expressions are discounting what's really going on internally with your kid, and, as a result, he or she just stops listening.

Instead, I learned how to use expressions with the "I"

word in it, such as "I worry when you come home later than your curfew."

Or, "It makes me feel bad when you ignore my instructions."

Over the past year, I've made a concerted effort to change the way I talk to Curly Girl and Cheetah Boy, and I think it's one of the reasons we all get along much better now.

These days, I try to talk with them, and not just at them.

But there are still times when I remember all the stupid things I've said to my kids, and sometimes recall my mom saying the same thing to me. Here are my top ten:

1. "Oh, hi, are you home?" Well, duh. I just watched her walk in the door. My mom used to ask me this, and I thought it was idiotic fifty years ago. It still is today.

2. "Are you planning to leave that on the floor where you just dropped it?" Of course he is. Whether it's a towel, a ripped envelope or a fork, once it's left his hands, in his mind, he's no longer responsible for it.

3. "If you're not ready in two minutes, I'm leaving without you." Gee, since the entire trip involves taking my kid to the doctor, he pretty much knows I'm not driving off until he gets in the car.

4. "Don't cry." No one in the history of the genus *Homo sapiens* ever stopped crying because they were told to stop, and, in fact, they may have sobbed harder, because now they felt humiliated, too. "Aw, come here and tell me about it" will work much better.

5. "Do you have homework tonight?" Of course not. Neither of my children has ever had homework assigned to them in their entire formal education, or, if it was assigned, they already "did it in class."

6. "Don't make me tell you again." My kids consider this to be a dare, because of course I will have to tell them again, and then I will be even more annoyed.

7. "Do you want me to get the belt?" I'm lying about that one. I would never say that to my teens, but sometimes I fantasize about it. My dad had a piece of leather on the top shelf of his closet that he intended to make into a belt someday. Its sole purpose for existence was to loom there as a warning to my brother and me. He almost never pulled it out, but he did occasionally threaten us with it. And, now, as a parent, when I'm just driven to the wall, I kind of wish I could, too. It would be pointless, though, because my kids would know I was bluffing. I don't even own a belt. Somehow, "Do you want me to get the scarf?" doesn't have the same sense of danger.

8. "How many times do I have to tell you that?" At least 1,811 more.

9. "Someday, you'll thank me for this." Or not. But maybe your future spouse might.

10. "That's disgusting. Were you raised by wolves?" I still remember saying this to my son when, at age nine, he begged to be taken to a particularly elegant restaurant. After a long discussion about proper behavior, I agreed to take him. And, when his steak arrived, he picked it up with his hands and gnawed on it like a baboon.

Apparently, he was raised by wolves.

# 8

# HOW'S YOUR HEALTH?

# DOCTOR VISIT TRIES OUR PATIENCE

SO ONE day, I left work early to take my kids to get their camp physicals.

We sat in the doctor's outer office for fifty-seven minutes, trying not to breathe the air of the children next to us, who were coughing like tubercular coal miners. Then, a nurse took the rugrats and did the whole thing—take off your shoes, get on the scale, stick this thermometer in your ear.

After all that, we finally got into the Inner Sanctum, where the kids got little cups to pee in and got their fingers stabbed to have blood drawn. They thought making pee-pee in the cup was kind of fun, but they were not in favor of the finger stabbing, which they indicated by screaming until they were hoarse.

Then, we waited for another fifty-six minutes in the tiny examination room, which quickly became like a cell in the Bastille.

Every thirty seconds, the kids demanded to know whether they had to get shots.

Meanwhile, I tried to keep them from A) taking all the tongue depressors and making a castle out of them; B) twirling on the doctor's stool until it comes apart; C) pulling the blood pressure monitor out of the wall; D) removing all the paper gowns from the drawer and making costumes out of them; E) grabbing a bunch of rubber gloves and blowing them up like balloons; F) yanking the stirrups out of the examining table so hard they break; and G) fighting over whose turn it is to lie down.

I tried to get them interested in reading the colorful, anatomically correct posters about pelvic disease and uterine cancer, but they weren't having any of it. Finally, another nurse came in and gave them an eye test.

Just when I was about to lose my mind, the doctor finally

came in and began reading the file. "Your kids aren't due for an annual physical until July," she announced. I explained how they needed the physical for camp, and this year I was actually doing it early and not waiting until the last minute.

I felt like stabbing her with a tongue depressor, but the kids had already used them to build Windsor Castle.

## ER CAN STICK IT IN ITS EAR

RECENTLY, for unexplained reasons, Curly Girl put a plastic BB in her ear. Surprise! It got stuck. She came running over, demanding to go to the hospital. It was in there too tightly for her to get out, but still visible.

Though it didn't actually hurt, she screamed and cried plenty, as if it were a hot coal in there instead of an innocent piece of plastic.

I asked her exactly how that happened. Did she think the BB could be fired from that position? And where was the air rifle, because I just couldn't see any reason for a girl her age to stick something like that in her ear.

I mean, come on, maybe a toddler. But a fifth grader?

She didn't really have an answer, but she did have a solution: Take her to the emergency room.

Now, this all happened on a Saturday night, and even if you've never been in a hospital in your life, you probably know that you don't want to be going to the ER on Saturday night. Not unless you have at least six gunshot wounds. Preferably with bullets lodged in internal organs.

Otherwise, you're gonna be waiting a long, long time. Also, my own recent trip to the emergency room, when I discovered I had a brain tumor, didn't make me all that anxious to return.

Instead, I told her to go find a pair of tweezers.

Now, I knew this quest was going to be sort of like looking for the Holy Grail, because no pair of tweezers remains more than a week in my first aid kit.

Instead, they can be found later in the flower beds, where someone was using them to pick up beetles, or in the front yard, where another child was collecting ants.

Meanwhile, my friend Barb, who was visiting, was looking at me like, "Wow, what a bad mother you are," and thinking to herself, "I would have taken her to the emergency room." She still remembers when her little brother Buzz got a lotto ball stuck up his nose and had it vacuum extracted at the hospital.

A sobbing daughter soon reappeared, stating the obvious—that no tweezers were to be found anywhere near where they belonged.

So I sent her across the street to the neighbors' house, and she returned with a useful pair. Obviously those parents have figured out a better method than me to keep them out of their kids' hands. I made her sit still, which wasn't easy with all the sobbing and screaming, and Barb held her head while I performed surgery.

It took maybe a couple of minutes to get the tweezers around the offending part and yank it out.

The sobbing and screaming didn't stop immediately, though I pointed out to her the offending object was NO LONGER THERE. I suggested maybe next time she should NOT STICK THINGS IN HER EARS.

Even though I was successful, I still felt a tiny bit guilty, because I know a lot of moms would have rushed their precious ones off to the ER

As a middle-aged mom, though, I am a big fan of my big fancy first aid kit I bought from the Red Cross when I did CPR training.

Did the kid slice something open? That happens

regularly around our house, since my kids are always getting into something they shouldn't. Patch 'em back up yourself. I keep this kit under the front seat of my car, and it comes in handy on trips, at soccer games, plenty of places.

The weirdest accident was when Cheetah Boy threw his sweater up in the air in Curly Girl's bedroom. It shattered the overhead light, which then cascaded down and cut his arm in several places.

However, none of the wounds was deep, so I did my normal procedure. Apply pressure to stop the bleeding, pour in disinfectant and, if necessary, use a butterfly bandage. That is all the doctor would do, anyway.

I was reminded of how much I dislike emergency rooms last week when Curly Girl had to do the mile run at school. She was extremely short of breath afterward, to the point that the school nurse called me.

I picked her up and drove her directly to the ER. No messing around with kids who can't breathe.

The awesome folks at the hospital got her into a bed right away and started her on a monitor. By this time, though, her breathing had returned to normal.

Of course it had.

Hours later, we emerged from the ER, with a promise to call her regular doctor. Well, that was fun.

The end result was that Curly Girl was diagnosed with asthma brought on by exercise. She has a cute inhaler now, and she takes Singulair at night.

So in this case, the moral of the story is: breathing emergency? Go to the hospital. BB stuck in ear? Get some tweezers.

Or, better yet, just don't put anything in your ear smaller than your elbow.

## I CAN'T HAVE A BRAIN TUMOR, I HAVE DINNER ON THE STOVE

I WENT to have a brain scan, because I've been having bad headaches. My doctor felt that I probably had a sinus infection. I agreed.

I don't know if you've ever had an MRI, but if you've ever watched a piece of luggage go into the airport scanning machine, well, that's pretty much what it's like.

After I had the brain scan, they told me I wouldn't blow up the airplane. Seriously, they sent me into this room where I waited for the results. However, my doctor was off that day, so instead of anyone talking to me about what was going on, a technician came over, plunked me in a wheelchair, and wheeled me directly over to the hospital emergency room next door.

Even though I am a trained interrogator, all I could get out of my ride was, "You have to talk to the ER doctor."

I pointed out to him repeatedly that I could walk just fine.

I had absolutely no idea what was going on. They stuck me in an attractive cubicle in the emergency room and took my vital signs. They told me to get into a hospital gown and get into bed, but I refused.

I wouldn't even sit on the bed, because I didn't want to pay for it.

"What the heck am I doing here?" I demanded of anyone who came near me.

People came over with paperwork for me to sign, admitting me to the hospital.

I was loudly refusing to pay any freaking $250 deductible for being in the ER and threatening to leave, because no one would tell me anything.

People just told me I "had to talk to the doctor," who

was possibly out having a smoke break, because he certainly wasn't anywhere near me for a long time.

Finally, after an hour or two of waiting, I phoned the doctor who was subbing for my doctor to tell her I didn't know why I was there, so I was leaving now and going home. I had to pick my kids up from school.

She told me I couldn't go home because they'd found a mass in the back of my head, and I had to wait for the neurosurgeon to come and see me and possibly perform emergency surgery that night.

Finally, the ER doctor deigned to drop by to essentially tell me the same thing. And on my questioning, told me that the tumor looked malignant so I should plan on being in the hospital five or six days.

"I can't have a brain tumor," I explained very carefully. "I have spaghetti on the stove."

This is what happens when someone tells you something impossible. It was like being told I had been abducted by aliens and was even now in an alien spaceship cleverly designed to look like a hospital. That seemed about as plausible to me as having a brain tumor.

I get a cold occasionally, but in general, I never get sick. That is why this seemed like an episode from *The Twilight Zone.*

Meanwhile, I was able to arrange for my friend Barb to pick my kids up from school. Other friends dropped everything and came in shifts to enjoy the pleasant fluorescent lighting, the blood pressure monitor, and other appealing amenities of my cubicle.

As you can imagine, my biggest fear was how to explain this to Curly Girl and Cheetah Boy without totally freaking them out.

Since I adopted them as a single mom, they are justifiably concerned about anything happening to the woman who gripes at them nonstop until they do their homework.

The ER doctor told me, "Tell them as little as possible."

I thought to myself, "This guy is cute, but he clearly has no kids."

If I told my kids I was abducted by aliens, they would want to know where and what time this occurred, what color was the ship, what was I doing there, what did the aliens look like. This interrogation would go on indefinitely until *SpongeBob SquarePants* came on TV to distract them.

After more consultation, I finally just decided to tell them the truth: that I had a lump in my head that was causing me headaches, and the doctors need to take it out so I can feel better.

I am certainly glad I decided to tell them the truth, considering that all the adults in my friend's house apparently were blabbing away around them about my prognosis. My daughter called me up in great distress, asking me, "Mommy, are you going to die?"

I assured her that I have absolutely no intention of dying until after I am a very old lady and have tortured her with years of arguments about why I refuse to go into the nursing home.

Then Cheetah Boy called me up in my little cubicle and said, "Do you have a tumor?" I said, "Yes, dude, I have a tumor. Tumor means lump. I have a lump. Like the ones you're always getting on the outside of your head from running into things. Only mine is on the inside."

In my attractive cubicle in the ER, the TV was showing a marathon of the *The Dog Whisperer* with Cesar Millan all day, so Rose Marie and I got a few pointers on taking care of Buddy the Wonder Dog while we sat there twiddling our thumbs for many hours.

The neurosurgeon came over then, after he just finished surgery, and decided I needed to have more MRIs and CT scans, so they shipped me over there.

The cute guy who took me up there in a wheelchair (even though I wanted to walk, they won't let you walk anywhere in a hospital, apparently in case you slip on someone else's blood and sue them) has three dogs, so he was happy to watch The Dog Whisperer, too, though he has a pit bull puppy, which sounded to me like a really bad idea. I didn't tell him that, though, because he was really young and cute, and I think he'll figure this out on his own.

After a bunch more tests, the neurosurgeon also decided that I wasn't going to blow up the airplane. And he thought the tumor on the back of my head looked benign. We danced a little impromptu jig around the cubicle. And after they shot me up with a bunch of steroids to take down brain swelling, they told me I could go home.

I was hoping to tell Cheetah Boy that they shot me up with the stuff that Barry Bonds was taking, but a male nurse (who clearly thought I was an idiot) informed me that Barry Bonds was taking testosterone. Oops. I don't need any of that.

There was a bureaucratic snag, involving getting an actual doctor who was authorized to approve letting me go home. That took three hours to resolve, but they finally let me go after I was a big enough pain in the rear and annoyed them all until they would do anything to get rid of me.

One of the hardest things is figuring out who you have to call to tell about this, because your closest friends would want to get a call from you, and not hear about it on the playground from the school bully.

But on Friday night, you don't want to be calling people up and bumming them out all weekend. And what do you say?

"Hey, how's it going? Oh yeah, somebody stole your parking space? Well, I have a brain tumor."

I just have to have surgery to get that nasty thing out of my head. The sooner the better.

And I'll share this tip with you. If you put on TWO hospital gowns, one in front and the other in back, like a coat, it covers your butt so you're not hanging out for the world to see.

## HOSPITAL HOSPITALITY: IF YOU MUST STOP BY, KEEP IT SHORT. AND BRING FOOD.

I THINK we can all agree that going to the hospital is a lot of fun. The lights, the aromas, the sounds. No wonder everyone wants to visit, it's like a luxury resort!

Okay, I'm lying. Being in the hospital is miserable for anyone who doesn't enjoy being poked, prodded, stabbed, swabbed, and awakened every night to inquire how much wee-wee they made.

And what about visiting?

It's easy to find out the hospital's rules, but that's only the tip of the iceberg.

For visitors, it's hard to know when to visit, what to bring, and how long to stay. For the patients, it's hard to say, "Get out!"

So based on my recent nine-day stay after brain surgery, here are my Frumpy Mom Official Rules:

**For visitors**
Call the hospital first.

When I was in intensive care, I didn't want to see anyone. I was having a series of really bad hair days, plus I wanted people to visit me later, when I wasn't doped up like a prize racehorse.

Imagine my surprise when I opened my eyes to see

—well, let's just say it was someone I don't particularly like. Someone who hadn't bothered to inquire if I wanted visitors—one reason I don't like her. And there I was, strung out on morphine and too weak to throw anything.

Really, some people just don't like hospital visitors at all, because they feel uncomfortable when they can't put on their game faces or war paint. Respect that.

Plan to stay only ten minutes.

I know, you feel like you should stay longer, because being in the hospital stinks, so your guilt makes you want to stay and stay, while your brain tells you to flee and flee. Really, the objective of a hospital visit is to let the patient know she's not alone, and that others are thinking about her, right? That only takes ten minutes. Then, get out. Unless the person pleads with you to stay.

Visitors are tiring. A friend of mine told me that his dad came home from the hospital exhausted, because he was a popular guy and everyone dropped in and stayed and stayed. He had to come home to get some rest.

Bring food.

Hospital food is nasty.

Call ahead and find out what you can bring to improve the situation. I remember one night, despondently pushing around some horrible cold replica of lasagna on my dinner plate, thinking of how it looked like dog food, and then, magically, a friend walked in with a huge box of brownies. This moment will live in my memory forever.

Another friend brought Thai food from my favorite restaurant, which woke up my moribund appetite and gave me a renewed reason to live.

Leave your kids at home.

Unless they're the patient's children, or saying their last goodbyes to grandma, there's no reason for kids to come to the hospital. It creeps them out, and they aren't wired for it.

Plus, they'll break the TV remote and climb in the cabinets.

### For patients

Get a gatekeeper.

Use a nurse or relative, who can kick people out gently or tell them to come back later. See if you can get Nurse Ratched to come in after a few minutes and order people out.

Don't let visitors tell you horror stories.

There's something about the hospital that makes everyone want to tell gross tales of other operations, other procedures. This must be nipped in the bud. Fake a heart attack and press the nurse call button. If that won't work because you're already hooked up to a heart monitor, interrupt and ask them about their kids or mother-in-law. That will distract them. Everyone wants to brag about their kids or complain about their in-laws. If these people are the type who can't be interrupted, get up to go to the bathroom.

Make up some really disgusting procedure.

You have to scare people away. "Oh, well, they're going to remove the catheter now because it has a lot of blood in it. That should take a half-hour or so. Oh, you don't want to stay? Okay, well take care now. Thanks for stopping by."

Be selfish.

You can just tell people, "Okay, I'm going to sleep now," and turn over. If they don't go away, cut them out of your will.

Finally, think about saving the visits for after the patient goes home. A woman from Ghana told me that when she gave birth, all she wanted was quiet time to bond with her new baby. Instead, her entire extended family crowded into the hospital room and partied around the clock, wearing her out. When she got home, and really needed some help coping with an infant, all of those family members had disappeared.

I told most of my friends just to stay away from my hospital room. This meant their obligatory duty visits were pushed back until after I was home. That way, not only did I have company as I lay on the couch recuperating, but I also had people to bring takeout, and available as personal chauffeurs when I needed them.

Assuming that your close friends and family have one duty visit in them, I recommend you force them to exercise it after you leave the hospital.

Preferably with brownies in hand.

## I'M BACK, BUT I'M STILL A FATHEAD

I KNOW some of you think I'm a fathead, while others of you just think I'm fat.

Well, neither condition changed appreciably during my recent trip into Brain Tumor Land, which included five weeks lying on my couch with a head full of staples, feeling like the Bride of Frankenstein.

Most of that time was spent watching the Food Network.

I wasn't very productive during this period, But hey, I can really make an awesome Thai curry now, as soon as I go to the Asian market and buy the thirty seven ingredients the recipe calls for.

Incidentally, while I was in the hospital, the nurses told me a lot of patients watch the Food Network, which seems pretty masochistic to me, considering what they give you to eat in that place.

But I digress. Back to the surgery. Numerous friends suggested that, while the doctor was in there, maybe he could fix some of the other problems with my head, such as my inability to remember the names of their children.

In fact, it's a drag that I can't use having a brain tumor as an excuse for my bad memory anymore. It was nice for a brief period to blame the rogue tissue for all my problems.

In case you're interested, the tumor was on the back of my head, above my neck, attached to the inside of my skull.

After growing for a year or so, it had displaced nearly all of my cerebellum, which is the lobe of the brain that controls movement, coordination, and blood pressure. I was pretty uncoordinated before the tumor, so you can imagine what I was like with it.

In the before-surgery CT scans, the big, nasty white blob is the tumor, and then after surgery you can see how my brain had already expanded back into the space a month later. Pretty amazing, really. I'm having some wallet-size prints made, by the way, in case you want one.

The best thing, aside from the fact that the tumor wasn't cancerous, was that I was able to regain all the function that I'd lost.

I feel pretty lucky, actually, because among the many people I heard from over the past few weeks were some whose brain tumors had a much greater impact on their lives. I almost feel guilty for getting off so easy.

The first time I sat down to use my laptop, I realized I'd forgotten how to type. But after a few minutes of tapping away, it came back. So I can work again. Darn it.

When I was finally ready to drive, I got into my 4Runner and realized I wasn't sure if I could do it. I drove slowly, as if I'd just gotten my learner's permit, until the full memories of thirty-five years of driving returned.

Too bad, because I was enjoying having all my friends chauffeur me around. I can also do all my own household chores again, which means no more food deliveries, sigh, and no excuses for the mess in the kitchen except that I'm a slob.

Cheetah Boy and Curly Girl did pick up the slack and do more chores than usual during my convalescence, but when they saw me getting better, as you might expect, it got harder and harder to get them to do the grunt labor.

This week, though, they've both gone off to Scout camp and left me alone (insert small teardrop here), so it's just me and Buddy the Wonder Dog to watch some R-rated movies and dirty up the house.

Little did I know that, ten years later, I'd be back in the hospital, this time with cancer. I'm hoping I'll be around to write another epilogue, in another ten years.

# 9

# GLOBETROTTING ON THE CHEAP

# PORN PLAYING CARDS
# AND A BOUT OF FLU?
# AW, SON, YOU SHOULDN'T HAVE!

SO REMEMBER when I sent Cheetah Boy to Europe? All he brought me back was a lousy case of the flu.

Well, he also brought me a pack of playing cards he bought in Pompeii, with pornographic images of ancient people doing unmentionable things in silhouette.

I would rather have a scarf.

When I picked Cheetah Boy up at LAX, I was impressed not only with how mature he seemed, but also with his deep, George Hamilton-worthy tan. In fact, he looked disgustingly healthy, especially considering he'd spent the previous night sitting up in the Stockholm Airport, begging me via text to put some money in his account so he could get some Swedish kronor from the ATM and buy something to eat.

When I come back from a trip, I look like a hairball the cat threw up three days ago. Cheetah Boy looked like he'd just come back from the French Riviera and the Greek islands, which, actually, was true.

I got the flu that he brought home, plus the deck of souvenir playing cards.

"Why did you bring me these?" I asked him when we got home, holding up the obscene cards he'd just handed me.

"I bought these for you in Pompeii," he said, smirking, knowing that I've always dreamed of seeing the ancient Roman city buried by an eruption of Mount Vesuvius.

The backs of the cards showed couples busily engaged in prehistoric pursuits, rendered in that stylized black design you see on ancient Greek and Roman pottery.

Cheetah Boy started laughing, clearly thinking the whole thing was hilarious, and I realized I'm unlikely to ever get a decent gift from him until he gets married and his wife picks it out.

I handed him back the cards and said, "Gee, thanks."

Then, he started coughing. And he kept coughing for a week, along with other less savory symptoms of his trip that I'll spare you, except to say no one got any sleep in our tiny house for the next few nights.

He got so ill that one night I found him lying on the kitchen floor, dramatically demonstrating that he was too sick to get up.

Since he's a bit of a hypochondriac, and none of us had slept for days, I showed my maternal tenderness by shouting at him to cut the histrionics and go back to bed, and, amazingly enough, he did.

Then, I started coughing and coughing as well, and I couldn't shout at myself, because I'd completely lost my voice. My kids appreciated this, because instead of yelling at them to clean up their messes in the kitchen, all I could do was whisper.

As my son unpacked, he showed me the watch he'd bought in Paris. With my money. And the Mercedes cologne he bought. With my money. At a certain point, I just walked away before he pulled out the Rolex and the tennis bracelet. He had a great time on the trip, despite having to pitch his tent and blow up his air mattress every night, and spend his days tossing on a motor coach full of other young adults.

But now he's miffed that he can't drink, because he became accustomed to having a beer with dinner. Sorry, my friend. You'll have to wait until you're twenty-one. Or at least until we go to Mexico, where the drinking age is eighteen.

Just try not to get sick while you're there.

# HOW TO TAKE YOUR KIDS EVERYWHERE WITHOUT TOTALLY LOSING YOUR MIND

WE'VE petted baby whales off the coast in Baja, rappelled into a limestone sinkhole in the Yucatan, gotten stuck in the mud in Canyon de Chelly, ridden elephants in Thailand, watched lions mating in Kenya, toured Windsor Castle in England, and used the water bus in Venice.

"Are you taking your kids?" people ask me when I announce I'm off to an exotic locale. Well, I am middle-aged and single, and I couldn't imagine going on a trip without my rugrats, even if hauling them along can be a challenge. After all, there are two of them. They outnumber me.

But because I'm now older and at least a bit wiser, I have some systems that make life easier when we travel:

### Get real

Be honest about how much you can really put your kids through. Children can only endure a limited amount of constant traveling before they go on strike and make your life miserable. On our recent trip to Italy, we were flying into Milan, in the north. My friend insisted that we had to visit Rome, even though that was a ten-hour train ride south. I refused. That was just too much for kids who had already endured a transatlantic flight. Instead, we all enjoyed the charms of Northern Italy, riding the water bus through the canals of Venice, cruising on day trips along brilliant blue waters of the Italian Riviera. Our longest journey inside Italy was a three-hour train ride from the Riviera to Venice, during which the kids had fun running to the snack bar and petting all the dogs on board. The children didn't even know or care that they'd missed being force-marched through the Vatican.

### Plan the trip around the kids

Listen to your children and think about what they like to do.

A member of my family who shall remain nameless, well, okay, he's my brother, hates Disneyland, so he never takes his kids there when he comes here to visit me in Southern California. Instead, he makes them do things he enjoys, like sweaty, grueling hikes or crawling through caves full of spiders. Surprise! Now that they're teenagers, they don't want to go on vacation with him. He can't understand why.

If there are elements they don't like, then bribe 'em. I'm not a big advocate of bribery at home, but on vacation, all bets are off. I mean, it's their vacation too.

I dragged my kids to Southern Mexico to study Spanish. They hated being trapped in a stuffy classroom each morning, so I bribed them. If they sat contentedly in class, then afterward they got to walk down to the plaza, drink hot chocolate with cinnamon, and buy a balloon from one of the many balloon vendors there. They loved it.

## Nix museums

Forget about dragging them through museums, if they don't want to go. In Venice, we ignored them. I know that's heresy, but the whole city is a piece of living history, so why do we have to pay a ton of money to go into a musty building the kids will hate? On that trip, their hands-down favorite activity was feeding the pigeons in St. Mark's Square. I spent a long time watching the kids play with the pigeons, sitting on some steps and resting my tired feet. When we came home, they told everyone that was their favorite activity.

In London, kids would like the British Museum, but just visit the mummies, the Greek and Assyrian rooms, and then get out of there. Instead, take the Tube through the Docklands, an exciting light-rail trip through modern London that feels like a theme-park ride. Get off at Greenwich, and take the tunnel underneath the Thames to the lovely green township, where kids can put their feet into two different time zones at once and run around in a beautifully green park.

Then, take a tour boat on the Thames back to the city. If you absolutely must go into a museum, give the kids sketch pads or a scavenger hunt list, and let them find the masterpieces. In England, I took the kids to Windsor Castle, so they could see a real, living castle where the queen lives part-time, But honestly, the only things they truly enjoyed were the Armoury displays and the Beefeaters. I'm not sure it was worth the NINETY DOLLARS we had to pay in admission fees.

## Take red-eye flights

Because it's nighttime and dark, the kids will be more likely to fall asleep and stay asleep. They're usually cheaper, too. And make sure there's something to do onboard. You can call the airline to ask if the flight you're considering has in-seat entertainment systems. It's worth the time to check. In a worst-case scenario, bring extra headphones for the airplane movie. We flew back from Europe on Alitalia, enduring the eleven-hour trip without any headphones to watch the movies, because they ran out! Can you imagine? I was annoyed with myself, because I usually throw a couple of extra headphones into my bag, but forgot. On the other hand, our eleven-hour trip from Taiwan to LAX was a piece of cake, because the plane was brand-new with personal video systems that the kids loved. It kept them entertained, and they didn't squabble.

## Rent an apartment

I'm sure your children are perfectly behaved, but mine are very rambunctious. It's much easier to contain their energy in a rented house or apartment than in a hotel. You also save a ton of money over the cost of eating out, and have a place to keep snacks and milk. Our recent trip to Italy was made possible because I did a home exchange with a family in Italy, where they stayed in my home and I stayed in their vacation apartment on the Italian Riviera. So not only did we stay for free, but we also had a kitchen to prepare meals, making it possible to visit a country that otherwise would have been prohibitively expensive for us. You can find exchange clubs and vacation rentals easily on the internet for anywhere you want to go in the world.

## Bring drugs

I always travel with a gallon-sized baggie of over-the-counter medicines that I know and trust. It's a pain to haul them around, but it saves a lot of time looking for a pharmacy where someone will understand the English word for ibuprofen. I also bring a mini-first aid kit including bandages, antibacterial cream, safety pins, matches, cortisone cream, motion-sickness pills, digital thermometer, and sanitizing wipes. On a recent trip to Thailand, I used the safety pin and matches on myself, to pry out a bamboo splinter in my finger and then put antibacterial cream on it, the thermometer to monitor my son's temperature when he came down with tourist tummy, the Pepto-Bismol to relieve his discomfort, cortisone cream for the heat rash the kids developed all over their bodies, the bandages on my daughter's knee when she ripped it open on a rock while snorkeling, and the ibuprofen on myself for enduring all of the above.

## Pack light

Anywhere you go, you can get laundry done. In some countries, it's dirt cheap and comes back folded in nice plastic bags. It's easier than hauling around heavy luggage. Give the kids their own pint-sized wheelie suitcases and backpacks. My daughter was three years old when she got her own tiny suitcase. I painted flowers all over it with her name on it. She loved it and wheeled it on many planes before it finally fell apart. We all travel with small-wheeled cases that can easily be transported anywhere, but I like to check them as baggage anyway. It's not worth saving twenty minutes to have to haul all that stuff on the plane, sometimes on and off multiple planes.

The kids bring two sizes of backpacks, one larger one for travelling, when they need to be able to put snacks, water bottles, and all forms of entertainment in it, the smaller one for walking around, when they just need a place to stash their water bottles and money.

I keep the following items permanently in my suitcase: a small night light for hotel bathrooms, a deck of cards, a travel alarm clock, a sleep mask, earplugs, safety pins, a soft synthetic money belt, a small bottle of ibuprofen, cough drops, a ChapStick, photocopies of our passports, and tiny rain poncho packs.

### Bring snacks
Ah, the tried-and-true trick all parents know. I bring familiar snacks from home, and as the kids eat their way through them, I replace them with travel mementos.

Now that my kids are older, I make them haul most of their own snacks in their suitcases. Then, I don't have to listen to them argue over who ate the last beef jerky. My kids have to eat every two hours, so a twelve-hour plane flight with only two meals would be sheer torture if they didn't have a backpack crammed full of Ritz crackers and Slim Jims.

### Throw out the rules
At home, my kids have to eat salad and vegetables, and don't get sugar or sodas. On vacation, I don't care. I'm not going to spend my precious vacation hassling with them over their diet. They won't get rickets before we get home, and if they don't try the fried grasshoppers, who cares? Ditto for TV-watching. If watching *The Wizard of Oz* in Swahili

keeps them amused, it's okay with me.

In Thailand, we stayed at a rainforest resort that provided three meals a day. Well, my kids need to eat more often. I set up a deal with the manager so the kids could go to the restaurant and order French fries whenever they wanted a snack, and they would add it to my bill. Do I let them eat unlimited French fries at home? No. Did I care if they pigged out in Thailand? No, not really.

On the other hand, I wasn't like an English couple we met at a Thai beach resort on Ko Lanta, a beautiful tropical island, who catered to their children's Western appetites to the extent that they took the kids first to the resort restaurant, where they could get hamburgers and pizza, and later to a Thai restaurant where the parents could get what they wanted. How are kids ever going to learn to expand their palates under those circumstances? There's always something kids will eat on the menu, even if it's only fried rice. If they eat enough fried rice, they might get sick of it and try the curry, which is exactly what happened to my daughter on our last trip. I'm delighted to say she's now developed a taste for mild curries.

## ROAD RULES
## FOR NAVIGATING TRIPS WITH KIDS

THE MOST memorable expressions of travel: "Are we there yet?" "I have to go right now" and "Stop the car, I lost my turtle" were all uttered by people younger than eighteen, on road trips with their parents.

The latter phrase was screeched by my eight-year-old brother in the back seat of our Ford station wagon, when the turtle he insisted on bringing on our trip escaped into the bowels of the trunk.

Buckets of anguished tears later, my brother's turtle was recovered from under a pile of sleeping bags, after our dad had unloaded everything from the car and piled it by the side of the road.

I've seen many miserable families on vacation who suffer from one of two opposite problems: They give in to their kids too much, or they insist on their own adult way of doing things. Clearly, my parents would have been much happier if they had not given in to my brother's pleas to bring his turtle on vacation. That is one nice thing about being middle-aged: I don't think my kids have to like me all the time.

On the other hand, I have friends who shudder at the words "road trip," because they still have post-traumatic stress over being forced to pee in a can because dad wouldn't stop his maniacal race across Kansas and Nebraska long enough to hit the head.

This is sad, I think, because road trips can be a lot of fun, if you prepare properly and have the right attitude, i.e. that of a benevolent dictator who rules the car but is willing to take requests from his subjects.

In our car, the driver rules. Period. Since that means me, I decide what plays on the radio or CD player. I am, however, willing to consider requests for radio stations, as long as the music doesn't actually make my teeth ache.

It's important to leave enough time for whimsy, or serendipity, or both. When I was a girl, my dad was a sergeant in the Air Force and we had no money at all. But my dad did have to go on temporary duty around the country. In the summer, he would cash in his plane ticket and use the money to drive us all to his assignments instead.

These trips were the only times my parents didn't bicker incessantly, and our dad, who always insisted on driving, was likely to stop when we kids saw the sign for the alligator farm or the petting zoo ahead and begged.

Allowing the kids to feel like they have control over some aspects of the trip turns it into more of a family adventure and less of a Bataan-style death march across the map. Our family always ate at truck stops, which is probably one reason I'm still large today. But it really carries the road trip theme to a new high.

The most important thing in a truck stop is that the kids have a few bucks to shop in the cheesy gift shop for useful items like signs that read, "Wanted: Woman with fishing boat. Send picture of boat." This gives you a crucial break from the kids.

I don't know how to break it to you, but twenty-four-hour togetherness isn't all it's cracked up to be. So decide in advance how much money they can spend on goofy novelties while you're at the table reading the Paul Harvey books for sale and eating chicken-fried steak.

Proper preparation is also a key element in how much fun your road trip becomes. Do a little research in advance, and I don't mean just talking to your neighbor.

A trip to the Auto Club can help you map out your route. Then, thanks to the magic of a little company called Google, you can see possible pitfalls along the way, i.e. how many alligator farms and "world's largest thermometers" where you'll be begged to stop. I also check out any local places to eat that don't involve the word "Denny's" along the way.

The most important thing you'll bring on your trip are the back seat DVD player and headphones. I know people who disdain them and say, "Oh, we play the license plate game and listen to audiobooks." These are the people who arrive back home looking like the zombies in Left4Dead2.

The downside of letting kids watch movies in the back seat is they tend to miss things along the road. I had to yank the cord out of the socket to get them to raise their eyes from their fifty-ninth viewing of *The Simpsons Movie* long enough to see the majestic moose crossing the road in Yellowstone.

"Cool," they said, then lowered their heads again.

I have actually solved this problem by banning DVD watching in any national park. National monuments are a gray area that can be resolved through skillful negotiation.

But the upside is so up, it's positively lighter than air. This was attested to by my friend Kim, who hates TV and doesn't even own one. Years ago, when my kids were little, I bought my first portable DVD player for the kids to watch on a road trip fifteen hours south into the Baja peninsula. My friend Stacey, who caravanned with us and her two kids in her own Jeep, did the whole audiobooks thing.

Kim was so opposed to our backseat DVD player that, before we left, she said testily, "Why don't you just drug the kids instead?" (Stay tuned, we'll get into that topic later.)

Kim rode shotgun with me in my car, where we listened to what we liked on the stereo, since the kids were engrossed with headphones and TV in the back seat. They only looked up every two hours to announce they were hungry or had to pee.

Later in the trip, Kim announced she would change cars and ride with Stacey and her kids awhile, to keep them company.

Hours later, Kim emerged from Stacey's car looking ten years older. She climbed back into my 4Runner and said, with great passion, "That DVD player is the best invention of all time. You should get a spare one in case it breaks down."

Told ya.

But about those drugs: I'll never forget the advice several moms gave me before my Baja trip, when I was worrying out loud about being in a car with kids for fifteen hours each way. The unusual aspect of this advice is that it was always whispered in my ear, after the other people around the water cooler had walked away.

What was the word? "Benadryl."

My friends wanted me to know about the wonders of this antihistamine that makes kids oh-so-very sleepy. But they didn't want any other moms to know they drug their kids.

Other modern inventions have also made road trips easier, such as air conditioning and Bonine, an over-the-counter motion sickness medicine that makes you less sleepy than Dramamine.

Though potty breaks along the road are standard procedure, try to count heads before you drive away. I'll never forget one trip, when I was maybe five. I'd crawled out of the back seat during a gas stop to use the restroom, apparently without being noticed. When I came out, the car was gone. So I sat down on the curb to wait. Sure enough, many miles later, my mom glanced in the back seat and discovered that her daughter was no longer sleeping there.

I could hear the shrieking five miles away as they raced back toward the gas station, looking for me. At least that's what I imagine happened.

Maybe my dad had just had enough of listening to us bicker in the back seat. This was, after all, before portable DVD players were invented.

## LEAVE ME ALONE, TSA

I'M NOT frightened of flying anywhere—except for the bad airplane food. But I do fear airport security.

Let me just say, I don't scare easily. Over my career as a reporter, I've covered gang shootings at midnight, stood in the path of raging wildfires, and chased crooked politicians down the street. As a mom, I even made it through algebra with Cheetah Boy.

But the friendly folks at the TSA and their foreign counterparts, that's another matter altogether.

I still remember entering the Cairo airport, returning from Egypt, when we were invited to pay a $20 bribe to cut to the front of the security line. This offer was made in whispers by the guy who manned the metal detector, who motioned us to come forward to where he was standing. Otherwise we'd have to get in the back of a huge, snaking queue, behind families who looked like they were bringing their entire villages, including donkeys, onto the plane.

Still, it made me mad. I don't pay bribes. So I started repeating the guy's offer to him, but really, really loudly, so the supervisors standing behind him could hear. Sssh, he kept trying to shush me. Finally, he shoved our entire party through the security gates, just to shut me up.

So that worked out, though not the way I'd planned. Then we had to go stand in more long lines to check our bags at Delta Airlines. I am not making this up—about every ten feet in line, they checked our passports again. As if somehow they might have expired in the interim, which would not have been impossible, considering how long we had to wait in that queue.

Then we were actually able to walk through the airport, until we got searched again when we went into the departure lounge to wait for our flight.

I must digress to explain that Egypt is a deeply conservative country where it's a bit shocking just to see a woman's hair. Even progressive, university-educated women cover their hair in public to keep men from being driven into a sexual frenzy. Nearly every woman is covered from head to toe, and they never meet a strange man's eyes, let alone speak to them or behave as if they might be equals.

So imagine my surprise when I stood in line to enter the airport departure lounge, and the grim-faced, Egyptian army guy in combat fatigues with the Uzi who was searching my backpack found something suspicious there.

"WHAT THIS?" he shouted, holding up the box of tampons he'd just removed from my backpack.

He pulled one out to inspect it, took off the paper wrapper, and kept peering at it, tearing the cotton apart while continuing to shout, "WHAT THIS?" at my face, which was now beet red and perspiring.

My kids, who were behind me in line, were convulsed with laughter.

The other hundred people in line, also flying back to the States, were pretending not to watch but really glued to the scene and smirking.

"WHAT THIS?" he shouted, even more loudly, as I tried to think of how to answer him without demonstrating its use.

Lacking any proficiency in Arabic, I had mostly been bumbling my way around Egypt using hand gestures to make people understand me, but I didn't think that would work here.

I kept hissing, "It's a private, personal lady thing." He just glared at me and kept yelling and holding it up in the air like a holiday sparkler.

At this point, the entire line behind me was shaking with suppressed hysteria.

"It's a LADY THING," I hissed again, feeling the blush spread down the entire length of my body. "A LADY THING." He ignored me.

Just when I thought I might be arrested for carrying illicit feminine hygiene products, a supervisor came over, whispered in the guy's ear, causing him to shove the backpack and its contents back at me with a grunt and one final unrepentant glare.

A nice final memory to bring home of our time in one of the world's most fascinating civilizations.

## THE TRUTH ABOUT WINE TASTINGS

I HAVE quite a few friends who are "into wine," which means that I get to drink a lot of pricey stuff without actually paying for it.

Some of them keep fancy wine chillers at home and invite me over for tasting parties. I like these people. I like them a lot.

Some of them take expensive vacations just so they can drive around and tipple in places like Napa Valley, where you can get stuck in traffic jams and pay $300 a night for a motel-quality room, just to wake up and say to yourself, "Hey. I'm in Napa while everyone else is at home trying to scrub grass stains out of their kid's pants."

I've been wine tasting in Napa, and many other places, too. And I do think any trip that consists of cruising around on scenic country roads and boozing all day is a trip worth taking.

But the thing about wine tasting—you never want to admit that it tastes like soap. Even if it does.

Because that will immediately identify you as a Philistine, i.e. a person who should be cleaning the wine-tasting bar with a rag and spray bottle, not standing at it holding a stemmed glass.

Instead of saying, "Hey, this tastes like soap," you have to look at your friends meaningfully, raise your eyebrows, and say something like, "Hmm, I detect a hint of raspberry and chocolate with a formaldehyde finish."

Okay, just kidding about the formaldehyde. You actually want to throw another fruit in there like cherry or, if it's a chardonnay, oak. It doesn't matter which one, because no one will contradict you for fear of looking like an ignoramus.

And what's with all these white wines that are aged in oak? Ugh. Why not just go out in the yard and lick an oak tree? If I wanted to drink wood, I'd get a wood chipper and a blender. And I'd pick mesquite, because I like the flavor.

I know I sound like I hate wine tasting, but I actually do enjoy it, especially at the less pretentious places where you don't need to hire a limo and wear a designer outfit to feel like you belong.

Once I had a blast tasting in Mexico's Guadalupe Valley, especially because the wines were all very affordable and the people were grateful you showed up. But then, I like most everything in Mexico except the drug lords.

The part I hate about tastings is after you've drunk their wine—you have to decide if you're going to buy some to bring home.

Because, to be honest, it usually doesn't taste any better to me than Trader Joe's Two-Buck Chuck (which is now Two-Forty-Nine Chuck, by the way). So I really don't want to spend $24 for a bottle of it.

That's why, even though I'm a certified tightwad, I don't mind tasting fees. If you're charging me six bucks to suck down eight ounces of wine, I don't feel that badly about walking away without buying.

Luckily, though, I usually have more well-heeled friends who will cough up the dough, so I don't have to.

Keep this in mind: A close friend of mine who lives in Sonoma, so she knows her wine, did a blind taste test for fun with her roommate, who worked for one of those ultra-snooty wineries that sells wine for $900 a bottle.

Okay, it's not really that much, but it might as well be, because I'm never going to buy it.

They literally did a blind taste test with Two-Buck Chuck, and couldn't taste any difference. And she actually worked at the place.

Something to remember next time you're filling your home wine chiller.

Now, I mentioned this to my friend, Brad A. Johnson, the restaurant critic at the *Orange County Register*. He's a guy who knows wines, though he's usually lucky enough to be drinking them on someone else's dime. A tough job, but someone's got to do it.

I asked him to do a rebuttal to this column and make fun of my ignorance. But he's too nice. Instead, he told me there's a real disorder known as "tasting fatigue."

"After sampling eight or ten similar wines in fairly rapid succession, the average person can no longer taste the difference," he told me.

You might remember from your Sunday School days the biblical wedding at Cana, where they ran out of the grape, and Jesus turned water into wine, and people then asked the host why the best wine was saved for last. So even back in biblical times, wine-palate confusion was a serious problem.

Brad told me he once went to "a wine blending party at one of the top wineries in Napa a couple of years ago."

Yeah. That's the kind of thing you get to do when you're a top critic. I only go to smoothie blending parties in my own kitchen, hosted by teenage boys. Guess who cleans up?

But I digress. Brad told me that he and the other folks were given several different types of grapes to blend to make their own meritage.

"I blended my first batch, and I wasn't happy with it. I blended a second batch, and I liked it better, but it still wasn't perfect, so I kept tweaking it. By the fifth or sixth batch, I was thoroughly confused. Of course I was drinking everything that I was tasting," he remembers.

"In my cellar, I now have a very expensive magnum of this wine I blended, with my name on the label, and I'm afraid to open it in front of my friends for fear that I ended up making a huge bottle of Two-Buck Chuck."

That's probably the only time I will ever hear Brad

mention cheap wine, since he's more the type who makes seasoned wine stewards quail before him in fancy restaurants. That's what he gets paid for.

I'm more the type that makes them chuckle, but that's okay. That's what I get paid for.

And, really, he shouldn't worry about his friends making fun of his wine. Even if they think it tastes like soap, they'll tell him it's got a hint of pineapple with chocolate.

## SO HERE'S WHAT HAPPENED IN THE GALAPAGOS

AN IGUANA urinated on my head. Something like that will not fail to get your attention, I promise you. It was just one of the more interesting things that happened to me on my trip to the Galapagos Islands, from which I returned a changed person.

So I learned not to stand under a tree full of iguanas, or the local Ecuadoreans are all going to laugh at you when the inevitable happens. This is an important life skill that I'm sure can be a metaphor for something. Let me know if you think of one.

Now, as I mentioned, I have cancer and just went through a year of treatment that wasn't nearly as much fun as it sounds. And I'm about to start some more treatment, that will last—well—as long as it works. This treatment might theoretically save my life, but it's also turned me into a major gimp. Let's just say I won't be running any marathons any time soon. Or watching them, either, if it requires standing upright for more than a few minutes at a time.

So, naturally, I decided this was the time to go to one of the most far-flung places anyone can imagine.

Well, what happened was that I discovered I could get

a very cheap airfare deal, which is the way most of my trips start. If I could get cheap airfare to Hades, I'd probably go there just to save money. I was able to use JetBlue frequent flier points to get myself, Cheetah Boy, and his girlfriend to Ecuador, which owns the Galapagos Islands. (Curly Girl couldn't come.)

We stayed in a very authentic Ecuadorean hotel known as a Courtyard by Marriott, and had some real Ecuadorean food from a restaurant called Wendy's. Seriously. We were staying in Guayaquil, which is the business capital of Ecuador, and very international. The nearby mall had a TGI Fridays. The kids actually got annoyed that the workers at Wendy's insisted on speaking Spanish. The nerve!

Anyway, after our South American odyssey at the Marriott, we boarded a plane to the Galapagos, 600 miles away and, two hours later, emerged onto the island of San Cristobal, which has a total population of 8,000. No Marriott here. We stayed at a cute guest house called Hostal Romy, owned by a retired fisherman and his family.

Now, many people assume that you can only visit the Galapagos on a cruise, but this isn't true. There are actually four islands inhabited by humans where people are allowed to stay, and we stayed on three of them. The cruises take you to uninhabited, remote islands where people aren't allowed to live, and you see the most exotic wildlife that way, or so I've been told. However, I get seasick, have no desire to sleep on a ship or be crammed in with lots of strangers, and I also can't afford the thousands of dollars that the cruises cost, per person.

When you stay on shore, you can only see the animals you can visit on a day trip—usually on a boat—and obviously you're probably staying in a town. However, I still managed to see every animal on my bucket list—sea lions, marine iguanas, giant tortoises, blue-footed boobies, land iguanas, a penguin—and much more.

Since I'm a gimp (remember?), I couldn't go on the fun hikes or snorkeling expeditions that the kids embarked on every morning in San Cristobal. I couldn't go biking with them to see giant tortoises on Isabela Island. All those things were too strenuous for me right now. In fact, I downloaded ten books to my Kindle, intending just to sit out in the beautiful equatorial sunshine and read every day.

I didn't read a single book.

Because the animals were just too much fun. Our guesthouse at San Cristobal (run by wonderful people) was only a block from the waterfront. After the kids ate breakfast and took off with their backpacks and snorkels, I would wander down, intending to sit on a shady bench and read looking at the water. Instead, I would always become occupied with the lives of the large and boisterous colony of sea lions who lived there on the beach and, sometimes, on the sidewalk and benches. There were lots of mothers, babies, and juveniles and there seemed as much drama going on as any good soap opera.

I would just sit and watch them quarrel, and bark, and bleat, and wrestle, and I was endlessly entertained, at least until lunchtime, when I, like the sea lions, would go find some fresh fish to eat at one of the waterfront restaurants. Then, I'd take a nap, and when the kids got home, tired and burnt to a crisp, full of stories, it would be time to (yay!) go and eat again. That was pretty much my schedule in the Galapagos, except on Isabela Island, I was watching the marine iguana families instead of the sea lions. And on the final island, Santa Cruz—sort of the New York City of the Galapagos with 24,000 people—I mostly just chilled at our cute hotel.

Something strange happened to me toward the end: I decided that this new immunotherapy is going to work. I decided to have more surgery to fix some things so I'll be less gimpy. And I decided to get well. Because I have things to do, people to see, and places to go. That's what happens when you spend twelve days basking in nature, away from the medical industrial complex.

So stay tuned. Let's see if I can make it happen. And if you want to go to the Galapagos, just go. If a gimp like me can go, so can you.

# EPILOGUE
## FINAL THOUGHTS (MAYBE)

SO THAT'S my story and I'm sticking to it, no matter what else you've heard.

I went from being a self-satisfied single career woman to an exhausted, anxiety-ridden yet joyful mother who discovered every cliché about parenthood was true.

And now that my kids are legally old enough to drink, I realize they can even be fun as bartenders.

At this writing, they're young adults and still living with me in my small suburban tract home. We continue to bicker over who's doing the dishes tonight, though I can no longer sit on the floor long enough to throw a tantrum.

It amazes me every day to look at them and realize what marvelous human beings they turned out to be, despite my best efforts to mess them up.

Nowadays, since I'm still in chemotherapy, they often help me get dressed and cook dinner for me, which they are quick to point out is the reverse of our earliest journeys together.

We just took a delicious camping trip together to Big Sur, where I stayed in a cabin and they did all the work, and I'm strongly in favor of this new method of travel.

If enough people buy this book and I'm not dead yet, I've been toying with the idea of writing a second book about our many travel misadventures, during which I have become famous for screwing things up so badly that they become a tale to share.

Meanwhile, thanks to my friends Samantha Dunn, Rebecca Allen, Barbara Kingsley-Wilson, Marilyn Iturri, and

Deborah Schoch, and my bosses at the Southern California News Group for helping this book happen. And of course, thanks to my publisher, Colleen Dunn Bates, for recognizing my genius.

And thanks to you for reading my book. Because you'll want even more of me after you read this (at least I hope so), check out my columns in the Southern California News Group newspapers (which at this writing consisted of the *Orange County Register, Daily News, Whittier Daily News, Pasadena Star-News, Riverside Press-Enterprise, Daily Breeze, Inland Valley Daily Bulletin, San Bernardino Sun, San Gabriel Valley Tribune*, and *Redlands Daily Facts*). And you can also join my Frumpy Middle-Aged Mom Facebook page. We have fun on there.

See you in the funny papers,